Main Trends in
DEMOGRAPHY

Jean Bourgeois-Pichat

Ruskin House   Museum Street

First published in Great Britain in 1973

ISBN 0 04 301060 1

This essay was originally published
as Chapter 5 in *Main Trends of Research
in the Social and Human Sciences*, Part 1,
Mouton/Unesco 1970

Printed in Great Britain
by William Clowes & Sons, Limited
London, Beccles and Colchester

Contents

Demography

I. GENERAL CONSIDERATIONS CONCERNING DEMOGRAPHIC RESEARCH

1. Trends in demographic research are affected by demographic development itself. All human sciences have this feature in common. The human being is caught up in the evolution of living species and the questions he asks himself, the explanations he seeks, the actions he hopes to accomplish are not the same, depending on the evolutionary moment at which he happens to find himself. Hence, in order to plot the course of future research, it is essential to examine what changes have occurred throughout the ages in the characteristics of the facts being studied – in this case the demographic facts.

2. Demographic facts are few in number and easy to define as soon as one asks oneself how the life of the human species develops. In the study of matter, for example, as research goes forward, new particles are progressively discovered and works on physics, published within a few years of each other, present very noticeable differences both in language and content. Nothing like that in demography. A work such as Moheau's, written nearly two centuries ago, on demographic phenomena contains the same headings as the latest treatises. To put it in another way, it can be said that in demography the real is immediately apprehended in its totality. By real is meant here, following Fourastié's conception, 'that which is or can be made sensible, perceptible by the senses ...'. In the sciences to do with matter, they are still at the stage of exploring the real, and it seems as though this exploration were likely to last some time. Both the infinitely great and the infinitely small seem to us to be limitless, which is why we refer to them as 'infinite'. Demography, and in general the sciences to do with man, are in the realm of the finite. The human being is the indivisible element forming the essence of phenomena, and when you have said that he is born, lives for a certain time during which he reproduces himself,[1] travels about, and finally dies, you have defined essentially what demography is about. Everything in demography can be reduced to those essential happenings.

3. This invariability of the language might give the impression of a static type of research. But behind similar expressions highly different contents are to be

found, and in this again human phenomena differ from phenomena of the world of matter. The electron in the Stone Age is no different from the one in the Atomic Age, whereas the family of Neanderthal man is very far removed from the American family of the present day. But there has been no break in the continuity between the two: one has merged gradually into the other, and there has never been the least hesitation at any moment in using the same word to describe them. Here we have the world of animate matter in process of evolution. These assertions are no doubt too cut and dried and perhaps, one of these days, it will be proved that inanimate matter, too, shares in a similar evolution. The electron of the primary age will then appear different from the one of today.

4. Demographic events set going phenomena of various kinds, and particularly biological phenomena at all levels – cellular, organic, individual, but also social phenomena. These last provide the occasion for group manifestations. On the occasion of a birth, a marriage, a death, or of someone's departure or return, the groups to which the individual belongs make their presence manifest and this manifestation forms part of a cultural system. These groups may either approve or disapprove of the event, may rejoice about it or bewail it – in a word, they judge it according to their own moral code.

Finally, because every demographic event is lived, in the first place, in an individual consciousness, it sets in motion the individual's whole psychological apparatus.

These three combinations of phenomena – biological, socio-cultural and psychological – possess different evolutionary speeds. Biological phenomena vary but slowly and a demographic event such as death, for instance, once detached from environmental influences, does not change much in the flow of time. All research has demonstrated that while the age-expectancy limit has increased, this process has been extremely slow. Such data as we possess which, unfortunately, do not take us farther back than the last two centuries, indicate no variation in this respect.

Socio-cultural phenomena are also very slow-moving, but they nevertheless have far greater evolutionary possibilities than biological phenomena; for whereas the available research data show the latter to be static, they offer us many examples of changes occurring in the former.

Psychological phenomena are obviously the ones which change most quickly, and it frequently happens that biology and the socio-cultural system are no longer adapted to the psychology of the individual, thus producing various kinds of tension. Birth control provides an excellent example of such conflict. It is decided upon in the privacy of the individual consciences, but more often than not it comes up against the survival of socio-cultural systems oriented towards uncontrolled fertility, and biological urges which it is not yet known how to curb.

5. This evolutionary possibility in phenomena which demographic events set going – a relatively important one if compared with that of inanimate phenom-ena – is not without having a certain influence on the characteristics of demo-

graphic research. It is true of course that observation can cause disturbance in the facts observed, so much so that the description given no longer corresponds to the phenomenon under investigation.

Further, if and when the results of demographic research become known to the populations concerned, they can, through a boomerang effect, produce changes of behaviour, a knowledge of the facts being one of the factors determining such behaviour. This is one side of the question which has been little studied until now but which should engage the attention of demographers in the future.

6. These relations between observers and facts observed determine to a certain extent the choice of the means of observation. They must be such as to disturb as little as possible the phenomena being studied.

Sample surveys fulfil this requirement. No doubt they disturb the fraction of the population under survey, but as this fraction is small, the disturbance of the bulk of the population is small also and it may be inferred that, on completion of the survey, no significant variation has occurred in the characteristics of the entire population.[2] Neither do observations derived from census returns of population and civil status statistics have much effect on people's behaviour. In this case they extend to the whole population, but are carried out in such a way as not to seem connected with demographic research; consequently they have little effect on the objects of that research.[3]

But it would be difficult to imagine, for example, a survey on the rate of fertility taking in the whole population. Let us choose as an example the situation in France. In that country, a law of 1920 regulates the sale of contraceptives. Sample surveys carried out with small groups of the population showed that 58% of the persons interviewed did not know that law existed. If, instead of such surveys, the entire population were to be questioned, obviously, once the total survey was over, there would no longer be many people left who were unaware of that law. The figure of 58% that would be obtained[4] would refer to a population of the past which no longer existed.

No doubt the above example is exceptional and the disturbing influence exercised by observer on observed has so far been fairly slight. If, as may be thought, however, demography ought to direct its attention to the study of individual motivations, disturbance is then likely to become less and less negligible.

7. Another uncertain quantity arises from the fact that demography confines itself to the study of group manifestations. The demographer's indications contain no precise information concerning a given individual's destiny. All they show is the possibility that that destiny will lead to such and such a situation. The result of this is that it is nearly always possible to find individual cases which are decidedly at variance with the average laws enunciated. These cases then appear to contradict such laws and this apparent contradiction sometimes leads, quite wrongly, to doubts being cast on the soundness of the demographer's conclusions.

8. The fact that the phenomena produced by demographic events should be endowed with memory is yet another handicap with important consequences for observation and, more particularly, the analysis of such observations. It is self-evident that a birth, for example, is an event which is lived in two individual consciousnesses, the mother's and the father's, and that it is something which can only be understood in relation to the past as experienced by those two consciousnesses and to the idea they have formed as to the future.

But when this birth is announced to the socio-cultural groups to which the parents belong, it becomes included in both the past and future history of those groups and enters into the social memory.

9. We must pause here to define more clearly the notion of 'history' as applied to demography, and, more generally, to the human sciences. The life of a human being begins at the moment the spermatozoon has fertilized the ovum. Twenty-three pairs of chromosomes have constituted themselves, bearing information which will make it possible for the individual to develop. This information takes the form of a certain number of genes distributed over the 23 pairs of chromosomes. It can therefore be said that an individual is constituted *ab initio* by a combination of genes drawn by lot, from a considerably greater number of possible genes forming the genetic heritage of the human species.

Let us suppose that the synthesis of a given protein is dependent on the information contained in a number of genes. If these genes are carried by the chromosomes of a single individual, that individual will manufacture the protein in question. But if, in the following generation, the genes are distributed among several individuals, none of these will possess *all* the necessary information for manufacturing the protein and no one will be able to effect its synthesis. Nonetheless, the recipe for this synthesis will not have been lost. In some later generation, through the operation of chance, and provided one is prepared to wait long enough, one can be certain that the right combination of genes for producing the synthesis will be found in a single individual who will then manufacture the protein exactly as his remote forbear did.

A similar procedure exists in the world of matter. For instance, in order to produce an atom of oxygen, a certain number of electrons have to be arranged in a certain way around a proton. If this is done in a different way, then you obtain something other than an atom of oxygen. It is possible that on certain stars conditions are such that the combination for producing an atom of oxygen will never exist. This does not mean that the matter composing that star has lost the recipe for producing oxygen. A variation in the conditions would be enough to enable oxygen to make its appearance.

In the world of animate nature, once a new being has been formed he possesses an individuality, he is going to have a history in the course of which he will preserve the impression left by events in which he takes part. The combination of genes which presided at his birth is his *essence*; subsequent events constitute his *existence*. It is in this sense that we shall speak of his history.

10. However, in the case of a living being, history is not simply an accumulation of past events, it is also – and perhaps especially – the consciousness of such an

accumulation; so much so that history is as much the future as it is the past. Certainly, for the living being, the present is not separated from the past, but he wants to be also a creation of the future. This quality, in a rudimentary stage in the case of primitive living beings, is definitely developed in the man who, no longer prepared to undergo his existence, insists on building it up.

No doubt it would be as well to recall here what we were saying just now about the evolution of inanimate matter and that of living matter. Essence and existence are probably to be found in all phenomena. But it is with man that the difference between 'being' and 'existing' takes on its full meaning, and that alone gives research into the human sciences a special orientation of its own.

11. Now, if it is true that every demographic event is a moment in a given life and can only be understood when re-inserted in the totality of that life, it is equally true that every such event is also subject to the influence of the conditions of the time. For instance, the death of a person depends certainly on his past life, but also on the sanitary conditions existing at the time of his decease. If he goes through some area where an epidemic is raging, he runs a far greater risk of dying than if he stays somewhere which is free from contagious disease. It is for demographic analysis to disclose and gauge the influence of the conditions prevailing at the time. Instantaneous behaviour then appears as the result of two sets of factors: those which only have a meaning in terms of a specific history, and those the existence of which is determined by the environmental conditions prevailing. It is essential to draw a careful distinction between them, for there is a great temptation to confuse the two. A lowering of the fertility rate due, for instance, to an economic crisis does not necessarily mean any lasting change in the behaviour of married couples. More often than not, their desires will not have changed at all. They will merely be putting off the birth of their children to a later date when the crisis has disappeared.

12. The variety of phenomena brought into play by demographic events gives an all-embracing scientific character to demographic research. Of all the human sciences, demography is the one that can least afford to do without the other sciences. We have already mentioned biology, sociology and psychology, but other disciplines should be added: political economy inasmuch as the human being is a producer during a part of his life and a consumer during the whole of it; ethnology inasmuch as behaviour attitudes are determined by cultural factors; ecology inasmuch as man lives in the midst of nature and is therefore obliged to enter into a kind of symbiosis with her, and philosophy inasmuch as demographic events possess a clear ontological significance. Then there are mathematics and statistics which provide demography with its analytical tools, and technology which, through modifying the environment, gives rise to new types of behaviour. Geography, medicine, history, law and criminology, theology, ethics, political sciences, educational science – all these are brought into touch at one time or another with demography. One can say that progress in any one of these sciences has immediate bearings on demographic research.[5] This close link with all the sciences is brought out in the language, as witness the various

adjectives that are frequently used to qualify the word 'demography', such as: economic, historical, social – or better still – psycho-social demography; mathematical demography (one also speaks of pure demography), population genetics demography, i.e. statistics, etc.

13. Despite demography's close links with the other sciences, little interchange takes place between demographers and other science specialists. The result is that the latter are unaware of the full scope of their own particular branch in which their researches would prove useful to demographers. It is to be hoped that this situation will change and that demographers and other scientists will be led to co-operate fully together. The present work might well serve to start such collaboration. The questions that have hitherto been left unanswered by the other sciences, because actually they had never really been put to them, will then be the ones that demographic research will take up during the coming years. We now propose to examine some of these questions.

II. DEMOGRAPHIC RESEARCH AND BIOLOGY

Population genetics

14. We pointed out just now how each human being, at his conception, was chosen haphazardly from among the multitude of genetic combinations possible, and how the sum total of possibilities formed the genetic heritage of the human race. But it is only a potential heritage; every moment we see how it is incompletely realized. All configurations are possible, each stands a virtual chance of being realized, but of course there is only one which is, in fact, realized... The individual can, by his behaviour, exert an influence on the materialization of this collective heritage: in the first place, by the way in which he and society regulate the choice of the marriage partner. Speaking broadly, there are two categories of genes: the dominant and the recessive. The character of each individual is determined by two genes (or two groups of genes), one proceeding from the mother, the other from the father. A gene is said to be dominant when it can display its character in one single dose, whether it be from the father's or mother's side. The recessive gene can only display its character if it exists in double doses, that is, if it proceeds from both father and mother at the same time. This explains the influence exerted by matrimonial customs. Consanguineous marriages, for instance, encourage the appearance of recessive characteristics, because the couple then stand a greater chance of transmitting to their offspring the identical recessive genes they themselves inherited from their common ancestors.

However, the individual can also bring his influence to bear on the materialization of the collective heritage through his own fertility. According to whether he chooses to have, or puts up with having, few or many children, the genetic information which he carries within him will be transmitted in a greater or lesser degree to the following generation. The differential mortality rate has a similar effect in so far as it concerns groups that are genetically different. We shall return to this question later on. The same can be said of differential migration, and for the same reason.[6]

The result of all this is that in populations the average frequency of each gene (or group of genes) giving expression to the information it bears within it evolves from generation to generation. The essential purpose of population genetics is the study of this development, or in other words, it endeavours to describe and to estimate the effects of different kinds of behaviour and different conditions of existence on the collective genetic heritage. It is a comparatively young science which calls for new mathematical instruments and which ought to develop in the years ahead. We find here a mixture of biology (transmission of genes) and sociology (differential marriage customs, fertility, mortality and migrations).

Here are a few examples of research in progress: to start with, theoretical research. We take a hypothetical case of panmixia, that is to say, a situation wherein marriages take place haphazardly within an inter-marriage area of given size. The average size of the family when the children reach marriageable age and the variation in that average determine then the proportions of consanguineous marriages.[7] Similar calculations are conducted by taking hypotheses other than panmixia. The application of these theoretical researches is to be found by reversing the calculation procedure: by observing the consanguinity incidence, the size of the inter-marriage area can be calculated. The manner in which inter-marriage areas – isolates, as they are called – develop and disintegrate has important effects on the health of the population, for while there are relatively few hereditary diseases, the organism always inherits a certain type of internal environment which can be more or less favourable to the incubation of diseases. Population genetics has hardly begun the study of all these phenomena, but it is a branch of demography which is expanding rapidly.

Intra-uterine mortality

15. But let us return for a moment to the fertilized ovule which has just started a new life – first of all an intra-uterine life during which it will be exposed to dangers such that, for very many this life will be a short one indeed and will end long before the birth of a living child. We know quite a lot about that intra-uterine mortality during the last months of pregnancy, which is known as stillbirth; but we are largely ignorant of what affects the rest of intra-uterine life. Strange as it may seem, we know next-to-nothing about intra-uterine mortality during the first month of pregnancy, and as for the succeeding months, our knowledge is confined to two or three tables referring to observations carried out in the case of a few thousand conceptions. That is not much in a world where each year there are 100 million births.

The question of male births has been discussed for a long time, but we do not know what makes for maleness at the moment of conception. It is thought that there are differences in intra-uterine mortality between populations and the various social groups belonging to a given population, but at present we are not in a position to estimate such differences – still less to discover the factors responsible for them. Some of them are biological. Actually, the formation procedures for new cells, from the initial cell onwards, remain fragile for some time afterwards, and changes in the chromosomes take place during the first months of pregnancy. The reason for some of them is known, but we are far from knowing the reasons for all of them. There are perhaps social reasons also, but all that remains to be discovered. No doubt during the next few years we shall have an answer to these questions. To know what happens between conception and birth is of capital importance. Only in this way may we hope to be able to guard against defective evolutionary processes, or even intervene in really serious cases.

The following concrete example will help to clarify this last point. We know already how to discover, before birth, certain changes in the chromosomes and it is possible, for example, to predict with certainty if a pregnant mother will give birth to a Mongolian child. Diagnosis is still far from easy, and the method cannot be applied to all the products of gestation, but perfecting the method is only a matter of time. No additional discoveries are needed and later on it will apply to changes other than those which produce Mongolian characteristics. In the name of what principle will it then be possible to refuse to carry out an abortion in the case of a mother who is known to be about to give birth to a deformed infant?

Infertility

16. Thus, sooner or later, the mechanisms set in motion by the fertilizing of the ovum come to a halt. If everything has gone well, they have been functioning for nine months and a live child is born in good health. If there has been any deficiency in their functioning, that child may have some deformation. It may be, too, that the gestation period ended with a miscarriage or a still-birth. Now, suppose we leave the child for a moment, well or ill-formed, as the case may be, to pursue its life in this world, and concentrate on the mother.

17. Up to then, she was fertile, since she conceived only a little while back. But when we consider a whole group of such mothers who have just given birth to a child, we know that all the time a certain number of them will become infertile, thus being unable to continue to procreate. And we know also that age is the deciding factor of this infertility. Even the person most ignorant of such matters knows very well that nearly all women are in a condition to procreate some time after puberty and that nearly all are sterile at the age of fifty. It follows, therefore, that progressive infertility must take place in between those two age-limits. But that is about all we know – at any rate so far as the present populations using contraceptives are concerned. We know a little more about populations in which married couples do not control their own fertility, whether it be the present populations of the undeveloped countries or, better still, the age-old populations of Europe. However, we know next-to-nothing about the laws governing progressive infertility with advancing age in the populations of industrialized countries, and in any case the causes of such infertility remain unknown to us.[8]

18. It is believed that genital diseases are responsible for the high infertility rate in some of the developing countries. But setting aside such environmental influences, a fact remains which has not yet been explained. How is it that out of the 750,000 odd ovules[9] present at the birth of a woman only a few hundred are used for fecundation purposes? And to what sort of 'ageing' process are those ovules subject? Obviously, the ovules which remain capable of being fertilized deteriorate in 'quality' as the mother grows older, as witness the increasing incidence of still-birth and congenital defects with the mother's advancing years. Lastly, how is it that this ageing process comes to an inevitable end towards the age of fifty? Here we have a whole field open to research in the coming years.

The spacing of births

19. Let us now turn to the women who remain fertile at the end of their pregnancy. It has been observed that they only regain their fertility after a certain lapse of time. A dead period intervenes in the production of progeny. While, however, we know that this dead period exists, we do not yet know much about the duration and causes of this temporary infertility and, here again, paradoxically enough, we know more about the populations in the developing countries than we do about those in the industrialized countries. It is known that breast-feeding plays a part in it. For the time being, all we can do is to observe the effect of this in a collectivity. It can be stated, for example, that in a population where all the women breast-feed their children for, say, two years, the interval between births is increased by about 30% as compared with a population where breast-feeding is not practised. But we are not able to identify *in advance* those women who will remain sterile, which means that the action exerted by breast-feeding on fertility is far from being understood. Genetic factors are certainly involved.

20. Let us place ourselves at the moment when the dead period ends and observe what happens. We will suppose that the couples do not practice contraception. The woman is going to become pregnant within a certain time which will depend on two factors: the frequency of sexual intercourse and the proportion of ovules of 'sound' quality. Indeed, it appears that, even in the case of a fertile woman, all the ovules are not capable of being fertilized. The woman continues to produce ovules, which is why she is not relegated among the henceforth infertile women. But from time to time she produces ovules that are not able to be fertilized. This amounts to a sort of temporary infertility, which is not bound up this time with any preceding pregnancy. The corresponding menstrual cycles may even be anovular, presenting all the characteristics of normal cycles, except for the presence of ovules. Such explanations are only the reflection of our ignorance. We know that something happens, but we do not know the mechanism. It is essential for the demographer to know whether the cycles during which fecundation is impossible occur at haphazard intervals or whether they occur in a series.

21. The frequency of sexual intercourse obviously does not depend on biological factors alone; social and psychological factors play an equally important part. Still, biology certainly has its say in the matter. Moreover, all things being equal, sexual desire weakens with age. But here again, we are totally ignorant of the mechanism of this weakening. We do not even know its extent. Information collected around 1950 concerning 6,300 American women and around 1957 concerning 600 Japanese women – that is all we have at present for the entire human race.

22. But especially the effectiveness of sexual intercourse depends very much on the length of time during which the ovule can be fertilized in the course of a woman's menstrual cycle. The length of life of the ovule, once it has been emitted, and that of the spermatozoa deposited in the woman's genital organs are combined in such a way that fertilization is only possible during a few days in each cycle. But we do not know how this combination is brought about, nor do we know the result. It it one, two or three days? The experts argue the matter without being able to reach any agreement.

23. We have spoken so far of woman's infertility; but, actually, it is the infertility of the couple which the demographer tries to evaluate, and which is the result of either the man's or woman's infertility, or again a combination of the two, with each partner able to be fertile in a different combination. One day the demographer will really have to distinguish between these three types of infertility, but that will necessitate a prior reorganization of the statistics. At the same time biology will have to enlighten us as to the mechanism producing masculine sterility and that of the sterility of the couple when each of the two constituents is fertile. All the biological problems connected with increasing infertility with age and with infertility at the beginning of puberty need to be studied separately as regards the male, the female and the couple.

24. The questions we have been led to raise in the course of this report concern all those fields in which the demographer – who specializes in the biological aspects of fertility – ought to direct his researches during the next few years. The World Health Organization clearly sees the importance of this, and has set on foot a research programme covering all these aspects.

Contraceptive practices

25. We have assumed that couples were not practising contraception. The practice of contraception is going to raise new problems. It is going to do even more than that: under its influence the very nature of the problems is going to be changed. We meet again with the idea expressed at the beginning of this report showing how man is caught up in the evolutionary process of living species, and how demographic events, by sharing in this evolution, change their nature through the ages. The populations which do not make use of contraceptive methods are far from using all the possibilities that biology offers them. By retarding the marriage age, and with the help of celibacy and sexual taboos, these

societies reduce fertility, and it may be said that at this stage of evolution, couples have the children that biology and society together permit them to have – but they have all of those. The individual has little say in the matter; he can only submit to the laws of nature and of society.

26. The practice of contraception has, in the first place, a quantitative effect, making possible the avoidance of a considerable number of births. But it also has a qualitative effect. Let us imagine a perfectly effective contraceptive. Then all the children who would be born would be children wanted by their parents. Their arrival in this world would no longer depend on a decision of society. This decision would be taken in the private consciences of the parents. The birth of a child, instead of being a socio-biological event, would become a psycho-socio-logical one.[10] This change in its nature would have important results for research; it would no longer be sufficient to know *how* births happen, we should want to know also *why* they happen. No doubt we shall still have to wait some time for a completely effective contraceptive. Still, recent progress in this domain has brought us sufficiently close to such an eventuality for it to have induced research to turn its attention to the question of 'why' births happen.

27. Additional problems arise from the fact that psychological knowledge is in advance of biological knowledge. These undesired children that are born willy-nilly, because we do not yet know how to exercise full control over biological phenomena, are at the origin of family tensions which ought to be studied.[11] The mere possibility of contraception can even be an occasion for discord between a married couple.

Further, the mechanisms which society has devised to limit the size of fami-lies have not disappeared for all that. Their continued existence can also be a source of difficulty. This provides a good example of the tensions resulting from variations in the evolutionary speed of the three sets of factors brought into play by demographic events – biological, sociological and psychological.

28. The manner in which demographers approach the study of fertility needs changing in order to take into account the above-mentioned factors. The tradi-tional method at present when studying fertility is to distinguish between mar-ried couples and others, and to pay particular attention to legitimate fertility. But, behind this distinction lies a variable which we have referred to above – the frequency of sexual intercourse, and it is because we know little about it that we choose, for want of anything better, to deal separately with married couples. In so doing, we divide the population up *grosso modo* into two categories with differing frequency rates for sexual intercourse, a lesser rate in the case of the non-married than in that of others.[12] But on the day we know more about the sociology of sexuality, parameters that are at present ignored will be seen to be fundamental. Whereas today we use the marriageable age or the age of puberty as parameters, later on we shall take into consideration the age at which sexual intercourse begins, and we shall draw distinctions between various types of couples based on the frequency of such intercourse. We shall also take

into account the age at which contraceptive methods begin to be used, and we shall distinguish between sexual intercourse that is sanctioned as opposed to sexual intercourse that is not. We shall also have to bear in mind the various contraception techniques, as well as the various ways of effecting sexual intercourse. No doubt the latter have a certain bearing on the efficacy of contraception.

Endogenous and exogenous mortality

29. Let us return to that child born alive, usually well proportioned though occasionally deformed, whom we left just now at the very moment he was starting life in this world. At the instant when the fertilized ovule begins its new existence, an ageing process is set in motion. During a certain time the forces of growth and of decay are going to co-exist in the same individual, then gradually the latter will gain the upper hand and lead him on finally to his death. But before this final event takes place, the individual will have to go through a series of crises characterized by a variety of biological disorders putting his existence in danger, which he will have to overcome.

That, *grosso modo*, is the sequence of biological phenomena that will accompany him from the cradle to the grave.

30. The causes of biological disorders leading to illness can be classified under two main headings: either the individual carries the cause in question within him, or else it is brought to him by the external environment. However, this distinction between endogenous and exogenous causes of disease is a little too arbitrary. A disease is always the result of a variety of causes in which endogenous and exogenous are mixed together. It seems that individuals have certain predispositions for contracting a particular disease. In the case of cancer of the lung, for instance, it is possible to distinguish between three separate classes of persons: those who are predisposed to this disease and will contract it even if they do not smoke; those who are proof against it and will not be affected even if they do smoke; and those who contract the disease through smoking but who can avoid it by not smoking, or, at any rate, by smoking less. Similarly, it is often hard to distinguish between a deformity due to some alteration in the chromosomes which occurred at the time of conception and one acquired during life in the uterus, due, for instance, to some disease of the mother. As we come to understand all these mechanisms better, demography will have to consider the re-classifying of deleterious factors, and it will no doubt be led to adopt a more subtle distinction than the one which consists in acknowledging only the two sets of causes – endogenous and exogenous.

31. In an endogenous disease, the deleterious factor can be present at birth in the form, for example, of a chromosomal alteration, but it can also be acquired in the course of existence, as a result of the actual functioning of the life-giving mechanisms. These two possibilities are largely related to two sets of causes of disease: deformities and senescence.

In the case of an exogenous disease, the ailment springs from an encounter between the individual and the deleterious factor. If such an encounter is successfully avoided, the disease does not occur, and for a long time health precautions were confined to that. The sole aim of public health measures is to protect the individual from dangers from the outside.[13] Progress in vaccination pursues the same object: vaccination cannot prevent encounters with deleterious factors, but its tendency is to reduce the effects of such encounters to a minimum. The disease ceases to be dangerous.

32. If, despite everything, the deleterious factor penetrates into the individual and the disease obtains a foothold, a return to normal calls for new methods of intervention. These have been lacking for a long time: the patient was left to recover his biological balance through his own personal efforts. The situation has been radically altered by the discoveries of the last few years. We know now how to cure, and we are getting better and better at it – so much so that we run the risk of forgetting the importance of preventive measures.

33. Public health measures are generally cumbersome. They set in motion administrative machinery that is often complicated and are only truly efficient when applied to the whole population. There is a great temptation, when cures can be effected easily, to abandon the difficult path of preventive medicine. It seems that we are now witnessing this tendency. The death-rate is certainly going down, but the disease-rate remains high.

34. There is thus a danger of creating a serious situation the consequences of which we are only just beginning to perceive. The reason is that the individual organism is a 'memory' and the person whom we say is 'cured' remembers nevertheless the ravages of the disease in question. We do not yet know if this 'memory' will not have unfortunate effects on his future biological behaviour.

35. A similar situation has arisen through the success obtained in combating the other category of diseases – those due to some deleterious factor the individual carries within himself, with this difference, however, that in this case it seems impossible for the time being at any rate to escape the consequences of our intervention, whereas in the case of diseases due to external causes we can still hope to be able to master those causes. There exist various methods of dealing with diseases due to internal causes. In the presence of a functional defect, there are several ways of trying to re-establish normal conditions. Sometimes a surgical operation is necessary to put the organism into proper working order again, or at any rate to get it to function differently. At other times, the faulty functioning of an organ is made good by supplying the organism with the elements no longer produced by that organ, or again, by ordering a special diet. But it is quite obvious that in solving a temporary difficulty the way is left open for further problems later on.

36. This is clearly shown in the case of a hereditary diabetic treated with insulin. An injection or the absorption of a number of pills a day enables the

diabetic to lead a normal life. Nowadays he is able to work, to marry, have children, whereas before, his activities were severely restricted, and having children was out of the question. But, of course, the daily injection of insulin has no effect on the genetic deficiency which can be the root cause of the disease. So, by allowing the diabetic to beget children, we encourage the transmission of the disease. The case of the diabetic is simply quoted here as an example, because it is the most striking and perhaps the oldest and most carefully studied, but of course there are many other similar cases.

37. All these cases lead in the same direction as the accumulation in the populations of individuals designated as 'cured', to whom we have already referred. These phenomena have made their appearance too recently for us to be able to gauge the consequences with any precision, but they already comprise a vast field towards which research ought to be directed in the coming years. This raises the whole problem of eugenics, which is stirring up very serious moral considerations.

38. All that we have been saying here about diseases applies equally well to those of old age, but the treatment of the latter has social and psychological repercussions which call for additional research. It is well known that the decrease in the death-rate applies particularly to youth. At the age when the diseases of the senescent begin to play a serious part, the decrease has been less marked, indeed, in certain cases, an increase has been registered.

Health priority
39. The problem no longer appears to be a medical one. Certain research work has shown what should be done so that the drop in the death-rate at this time of life should continue. The main factors responsible are obesity, high blood-pressure, too rich a diet, the consumption of alcohol and the immoderate use of tobacco. This means, of course, changing the whole way of life if a continued lowering of the death-rate is desired. It does not seem as if man were socially and psychologically ready to accept such changes. To do everything possible to save a human life is a basic principle of the present-day morality of humanity, but it would seem to apply only to the moment when the danger of death becomes manifest.

40. For instance, it is assumed that an inveterate smoker suffering from cancer of the lung has every right to expect society to do its utmost to cure him. But this same smoker bears a certain responsibility for what has happened to him, and if he calls on society to help him in the last phases of the disease which finally causes his death, surely society would have had every right to require him to change his way of life during the preceding phases of the development of his disease. Here we come up against a source of dispute which ought to engage the future attention of research.

41. We can observe here a change in the way of regarding questions of mortality different from the one we noted in fertility cases. Fertility, which is determined

by biological and social causes, has become something depending for the most part on psychological factors. Mortality, on the other hand, has become an occurrence concerning which society has more and more to say. The progress of medical science enables us to cope better and better with diseases, the causes of which lie within the individual himself. However, the therapeutic treatment is so expensive that there is a danger of no longer being able one day to give everyone the benefit of such treatment. Society comes up against an economic obstacle in applying the principle referred to above, according to which everything must be done to save a human life. Perhaps it will be obliged to choose between free medical care for all and, for example, the motor-car and colour television. Naturally, everything will still be done to restore the would-be suicide to life. The condemned man will still be given the medicines his body may require, even on the eve of his execution. Mother and child in danger of death as the result of an attempted abortion will still be saved, and the driver of a motor-car who has been hurt in an accident for which he is responsible will receive just as much medical attention as his victims. Attacker and attacked will continue to find themselves next to each other in hospital. But all these are exceptional cases, as can be seen, resulting from some sudden crisis, and their relatively small number has no perceptible impact on a country's economy.

The demands connected with the treatment of old people's diseases will be of an altogether different order. They will present themselves more and more frequently until in the end they become part of the daily routine, and an important fraction of economic activity will then have to be devoted to meeting them.

If the burden becomes too heavy, a series of choices will have to be made; as a rule these will be anonymous, and will be effected by means of credit allocations. At the executive level, regulations will inevitably be inhuman.

Our society has not been morally prepared for the advent of this age of social mortality and the whole subject calls for research. This is certainly beyond the scope of the demographer, but he could make a useful contribution thereto.

42. Purely economic considerations concerning the 'cost of human life' would no doubt be of help in reaching a solution, despite the fact that many illusions exist about this way of presenting things.

Economic development has no memory: the present and future alone count in its scheme of things. If a factory which has been 90% built shows itself economically useless, interest dictates that construction be stopped forthwith. The same applies to a human being. Whatever may have been spent on his training in the past, his economic usefulness has to be judged according to the present and future situations.

43. We have pointed out how the priority accorded by humanity to the saving of human life might be questioned if the notion of individual responsibility in the series of events leading finally to death were more broadly interpreted. It seems unrealistic to isolate the final event and leave out of account the events which have led up to and explain it, and in which individual responsibility often

plays a very large part. For instance, if it were definitely proved that by living in a certain way certain situations leading to death could be avoided, it would be difficult to insist on society's providing unconditional aid for all those who voluntarily decided not to live in the prescribed way. The return to a view of mortality as resulting from an individual decision could help to solve the conflict already referred to between the various aims of social and economic development.

44. We have just propounded implicitly the relations between morbidity and mortality. It is rather surprising that, while in dealing with the question of birth the demographer has set out to distinguish between the results of various factors – marriage situation, infertility, spacing of births, frequency of sexual intercourse, etc. – he should never have made any serious attempt to study the process leading from disease to death as a whole. This is something which demographic research should undertake immediately.

Progress to be expected in biology
45. Hitherto we have discussed the problems confronting the demographer due to the biological development of the human race as at the time this report was written (May 1968). We have not described the changes in biology that are likely to take place in the years immediately ahead. It is always dangerous to try to imagine the evolution of a science from the sole point of view of another science. We shall, therefore, restrict ourselves to a few remarks.

Completely effective contraception
46. The most striking progress – which is very likely to produce fairly quick results – has been achieved in the placing at the disposal of couples contraceptives that are being continually improved and easier to use. Consequently, we are going to witness a rapid change-over from social fertility to individual fertility, as described above. It is therefore going to become more and more essential to understand the 'whys' of conception. The impact on the developing countries will be considerable, but the essential change will occur in the actual evolution of the human race which will then follow a new direction.

The choice of sex
47. A more long-term development which could take place is the parental ability to choose the child's sex at the time of conception. The solution of this problem is unlikely to present any serious difficulties to biological research. The importance of being able to make such a choice is obvious for stock-raising purposes, and there, no doubt, the problem will first of all be solved. Extending it to the human race will quickly follow. It is hard to foresee the consequences of such a discovery. If it were found that certain peoples showed a marked preference for one of the sexes, the demographic balance in those countries could be clearly upset, and no government could afford to disinterest itself in the matter. Recent sociological developments in the study of the process of decision will here find their natural application. It is for the demographer to

hasten to indicate the consequences which any big increase in the proportion of male births, as compared with the present proportion of 51 boys to 49 girls, could have on the development of populations in the various countries. There is also the possibility that the percentage of males could be at the mercy of changes in fashion.

In the past, certain populations, by resorting to infanticide, have already carried out such a choice of sex, and the difficulties they have encountered offer an indication of what a choice at the time of conception could entail. Certain tribes of Eskimos which saw in the male infant a potential hunter and in the female infant a useless mouth to feed, have resorted to the systematic killing of girls at birth. Obviously, this brought about an imbalance between the sexes which no longer enabled the population to reproduce itself.

The mastery of old age

48. In a still longer-term development, one can look forward to the discovery by biology of the mechanisms of the ageing of the organs. The ageing of each individual begins at the precise moment when the ovule is fertilized by the spermatozoa. It presents itself as a kind of successive forgetfulness of the biochemical cycles built up on the basis of the information contained in the genetic heritage. The child who has just been born can already no longer produce certain substances which he manufactured perfectly well in his mother's womb. Thus the life of an individual can be viewed as the perpetual creation of new machinery for replacing older machinery which no longer works and which he no longer knows how to build. Death happens when the inventive faculty itself ceases.

Such are the apparent facts. But what is the profound reason for this non-remembrance which forces the individual to keep on inventing in order to survive? We do not know. Biology has set about trying to solve the problem and we may expect that a solution to it will emerge progressively in the course of the next century.

From the demographic point of view, the chief result will be the progressive disappearance of old-age diseases and, consequently, the postponement of endogenous mortality. This will have little effect on population growth, but considerable effect on its age composition. Whereas hitherto the lowering of the death-rate has scarcely had any effect on the age composition, the disappearance of endogenous forms of death will result in a noticeable increase in the percentage of old people, with economic and social consequences of which there is no need to remind the reader.

Infertility overcome

49. Suppose we go even further? We are then in science fiction. There is a phenomenon which is connected with the ageing process: the progressive development of female infertility between puberty and the menopause. A better knowledge of the causes of old age will no doubt enable us to understand better how it is that woman loses her reproductive powers, and then perhaps to prevent her from losing them. However, we must face the fact that here we are dealing

with complex phenomena which go far beyond those set in motion by the mere ageing of the organism.

The demographic consequences would be far-reaching. The ability to have children after the age of fifty would make it possible to build up a family in successive stages: for instance, two children between 20 and 24 and two more between 50 and 54 years of age, and possibly with different marriage partners. However, four children per family would constitute a very high fertility rate which, if applied to all women, would very soon lead to intolerably high population densities. Consequently, society would have to take steps to prevent a certain number of women from having that second family after the age of 50, even if they should desire it. We would thus go back – partly at any rate – to a social fertility situation, allowing only the first family, for example, to decide for itself in perfect freedom, thanks to the discovery of efficient and easily used contraceptives.

50, We could cite a good many more biological developments that would have important demographic repercussions. If, for instance, it became possible to transplant a fertilized human ovule into the body of a mammal for gestation purposes, the whole institution of the family would be upset.

If a method could be discovered for changing the genetic heritage artificially and creating new beings by intervening at the level of molecular biology, the whole evolutionary process of living species would be transformed.

It is for science fiction to put these questions to us, but it remains for the demographer to gauge their results on population development.

III. DEMOGRAPHIC RESEARCH AND ECONOMIC DEVELOPMENT

51. We have spent a long time on the biological aspects of demographic events. This is not surprising. As we have already said, the human being is only the last link in a long chain of living beings that have gone before him and prepared for his arrival. It is he who has taken the phenomena of reproduction and old age out of pure biology, though of course they remain, in essence, biological phenomena. It is by prolonging them existentially that they become economic, social and cultural phenomena. Let us examine the human being's economic activities first.

52. Man is a consumer and a producer of goods and services. Before the agricultural revolution, he was content to consume whatever the earth provided for him. Agriculture turned him into a producer and mankind organized itself in what is called a subsistence economy, whereby products are consumed on the spot, or practically so, by the producers, or at any rate all those either directly or indirectly associated with production.[14] There is no intermediary between men and goods and services. Money, by enabling goods and services to be exchanged, ushered in an important development and thenceforward a market economy took the place of the subsistence economy.

From a consideration of the new kinds of relationship thus established between products a new science was born, namely, political economy. But in the process, man himself disappeared. Henceforth, money was to become the unit of measurement, and all one had to do was to get enough of it for oneself in order to realize one's heart's desire. But this conception of economy left out of account the fact that, on the individual plane, man moves in a finite world and that whatever is seized momentarily thanks to the power of money is only done by taking it away from others.

A whole new political economy in which men would replace money as the unit of accountancy remains to be thought out, and here the demographer can be of considerable aid to the economist. Moreover, it will be from more than just a collaboration between these two branches of science alone that the new political economy will emerge. We are only now beginning to hear its first uncertain utterances.

53. It is in a planned economy that one is better able to understand the rôle of demography, and so that is the situation in which we shall first place ourselves. We will follow the planner in his preparation of an economic and social development plan by trying to show the help the demographer will give him. We shall then see how the type of research undertaken by the demographer can also be of considerable use in a non-planned economy.

54. Economic development is in the first place a question of the production of goods and services, and it is in view of certain more or less precise production goals that a country's economic activity is organized. These goals are fixed in relation to needs, that is to say, patterns of consumption. The elaboration of such patterns is a matter for the experts in the various fields. For instance, the nutrition expert fixes the food patterns, the architect the housing patterns, and the town-planner the dwelling conditions. These three examples have been chosen from among a number of others because they represent three specific classes of consumer goods:

a. goods and services consumed by the individual, or rather, the consumption patterns of which depend on individual characteristics;
b. goods and services consumed by the household, and
c. goods and services consumed by the collectivity.

Naturally, each of the above classes includes a greater number of goods and services than those we have just indicated.

Demographic variables have some influence on the fixing of patterns, but are not among the most important factors to be considered. It is obvious, however, that the needs of a collectivity depend on its age composition and also on the fertility and death rates.[15] Similarly, the household consumption of goods and services depends on the demographic characteristics of the households concerned (their size and composition). Finally, certain individual nutritional needs are closely related to fertility and mortality rates. But, above all, each average class for which a consumption pattern is fixed by the expert is, more often than not, self-designated in relation to demographic characteristics, viz. children, adults, the aged, workers, pregnant women, newly-weds, sick persons, aliens, household, family, village, etc. Hence collaboration is obviously necessary between the various experts and demographers, for these latter alone are able to give the number of units of each category, thus making it possible to pass from average individual needs to global needs, that is, to the global production necessary in order to satisfy those needs.

Population censuses provide the answers in all ordinary cases, but there always remain classes of consumers that have escaped the census and whose numbers have to be calculated. The demographer is relied on to supply such estimates.

Demographic prospects

55. Comparing needs with possibilities, the planner generally finds that the former are greater than the latter and he draws up a plan of investment designed to reduce the difference, hoping to eliminate it altogether in due course. However, as a rule, this final goal is found to be out of reach within a strictly limited time, and plans are spread over a period of years. All investment implies saving of some kind,[16] that is to say, a restraint on consumption, and if this restraint is too severe, the population feels itself to be under compulsion. Where there is a difference between needs and possibilities, the shorter the duration of the plan the greater the compulsion necessary. Consequently, this duration will be in terms of the capacity of the population to suffer, and the planner will, as a rule, prepare several plans of varying duration, leaving it to the political authorities to decide which one will not go beyond the point acceptable to the population.

In the case of each of these plans, it is indispensable to know what the needs will be throughout its entire duration, and it is here that the demographer again has his part to play, for he must be able to calculate not only the existing numbers of the various classes of consumers, but also those for the years immediately ahead.

Prospective calculations have led to the invention of special methods which now form an important side of demography: the calculation of demographic prospects, or again, of population projections. For a long time we were satisfied with very simple calculations, such as population prospects according to age and sex. Lately we have undertaken the calculation of prospects more useful to the planner, dealing with households, families, school population, urban population, etc. However, this is only a beginning and the field of activity is vast. With electronic computers it is now possible to deal with sectors into which, without them, we have so far been prevented from going. They also enable us to vary our assumptions.

Working population prospects

56. Assuming that the means of production are there, they then have to be used, and for that we need labour. The investment plan will have to be set out in terms of man-power and not confined to planning the building of factories and manufacture of machines. It will also have to show the number and the structure of the working population required to turn the means of production to ac-

count, and this brings us to a special side of the demographic perspective – the working population.

At any given moment, the working population can be divided into four concepts:

a. the working population corresponding to the aims of the plan;

b. the working population corresponding to the training which could be given by the various existing types of instruction;

c. the working population corresponding to the training actually received. This training is not necessarily that which corresponds to the training possibilities, for it is the combined result of such possibilities and of the use that is made of them. Everything may be on hand for training notaries, but if that profession is disdained by the population, the schools will remain empty and there will not be any notaries;

d. the working population corresponding to the termination of the plan, that is, when needs have been satisfied.

Of all these working populations, only the third has any real existence. But the calculation of the other three is a rewarding exercise. They must not differ too much from the third one, otherwise they give rise to tensions that are responsible for all kinds of troubles. And if the differences are too great, it may become necessary, as a result, to rearrange the development plan.

It is the task of the demographer, with the assistance of the economist, the teacher, and technicians representing the various branches of production, to calculate the above possibilities. We are still only at the experimental stage, but there is no doubt that this branch of demography is going to be developed very rapidly in the course of the next few years. The interpretation of these prospects is certainly difficult. The relationship between the training of producers and the aims of production is not a relationship in the sense in which that word is employed in mathematics, or even in the natural sciences. A given type of training does not correspond to one single class of production but to a whole range of production which means that there exists an uncertain quantity in production which corresponds to a given type of training. This is just as well, moreover, for this uncertain quantity makes it possible for technical progress to take place without becoming too inhuman.

57. So long as a large part of the economy requires only a relatively unskilled labour force, the question of training is not of any great moment. But with technical development and the increasing activities of services connected with teaching, culture and health, the finding of trained personnel is going to depend more and more on the number of suitable persons available for training. The discovery of such persons sufficiently early so that their talents can be made to serve the aims and objects of the economic development plan will then become an essential task calling for the collaboration of teachers, economists, demographers, psychologists and sociologists.

Regional prospects

58. We will assume that the development plan has been chosen. If everything

has been properly organized, the desired means of production and the workers to make use of them are available. This means that in the end the goods and services planned are placed at the disposal of the population. It is still essential, however, that these goods and services should be made available to consumers where the latter happen to be; so it is obviously necessary that the plan should have provided for a distribution of products that corresponds to the population distribution within the country. In this, demography has a clear rôle to play, and the capacity to view events in their proper light required of it just now on a national scale for various classes of consumers will be wanted this time on a regional scale, even down to that of the small administrative district. The mobility of man has a fundamental influence on the way in which he settles into the outside environment. He can produce, consume and spend his leisure time in different places. To pass from production to consumption requires, therefore, a knowledge of these migrations. A study of them is demographically important. We shall return to this question in a moment.

The distribution of currency

59. In a market economy, however, it is still not enough to have the necessary quantity of goods and services available in the places where the consumers are; the latter must still to be able to buy them, and for that they must have money. So it will be impossible to carry out the plan properly unless an adequate distribution of currency has been arranged for.

The three ways of acquiring money

60. There are three principal ways in which a person can obtain money: in remuneration for work done, as income from capital and, lastly, through payments effected by a collectivity and, more especially, by the State in accordance with existing legislation. The proportions of these three means vary, depending on the country and the political régime. Income from capital, while practically non-existent in Marxist economies, is about at its maximum in countries such as the United States of America. It seems that it is not possible for such income to exceed one quarter of a country's gross national product. A nation's capital represents four or five times that product, which makes it possible with a rate of interest[17] of 4 to 5 % to distribute by this means 25 % at most of the monetary resources placed at the disposal of the public.[18]

The proportion distributed by collectivities also varies considerably, depending on the country. It is large wherever the development plan stresses the social aspects of the situation. This procedure has been very much developed in the recent past in support of a policy of the redistribution of income.

Finally, there is remuneration for work done, which accounts for the largest proportion.

Behind all this monetary machinery, there is man himself. The worker receives in principle, in exchange for his work, the money necessary for obtaining the goods and services he and his family consume. But this does not mean that the other two means lie outside his scope. On the other hand, persons who do not form part of the labour force have only those two means at their disposal.

Capital income

61. The income from capital has automatism on its side. It is levied at a stage in production such that the worker does not receive the impression that what belongs to him is being taken away, whereas the money distributed by collectivities is derived in large part[19] from direct or indirect taxation submitted to rather than voluntarily accepted.

However, the income from capital acts in blind fashion most of the time and often is not channelled towards the persons who are in greatest need of it – those who do not form part of the labour force. The whole population shares in the ownership of capital, including members of the labour force, and it is often they who are in the best position to benefit from it. This drawback is mitigated by the proportion which this procedure places in the hands of collectivities. The latter, by serving as intermediaries, influence the distribution of income, but the proportion accruing to them is small. The system of inheritance adds further to the dilution of capital income among the population in general, a dilution which is again offset in this case by probate duties levied by the State.

This dilution among the population is far from presenting only drawbacks. Indeed, the possession of capital goes far beyond the right to receive an income from it. Owners of capital can bring great influence to bear on the economy and it would be dangerous were they to belong to one class of persons only, as, for example, the aged. Besides, it seems hardly desirable that ownership of capital should be out of contact with the labour force.

If we add that with this procedure it is impossible to distribute more than 25 % of the total currency placed at the disposal of the private citizen, recourse to the third procedure would seem to be imperative.

62. It is none the less true that currency distribution effected through paying an interest on capital is the method in use in numerous countries. The mechanism, the working of which we have just outlined, is not very well understood, but its connexion with demographic variables is clear. Marriage conditions, fertility, death-rate – all these have an influence on the way in which capital is distributed between the different generations, and the legal methods used in this distribution have a reciprocal effect on demographic variables. This is a sector which seems to have been unjustly neglected by demographers, and by economists also. It is true that we lack precise data, and the patterns we can imagine very quickly become complicated. So far, mathematical demography has failed to undertake a systematic study of the relationship between the generations. One of the results of controlling the endogenous death-rate will be the accumulation of capital in the hands of the aged. Although from a social point of view we can congratulate ourselves on this evolution, seeing that the money goes precisely to those who no longer receive a wage in exchange for work done, we are entitled to be apprehensive about the effects which this concentration of capital is bound to have on the investment policies in the various countries. With the future evolution of the death-rate these questions can be expected to become one of the main studies of demographers and economists.

Payments effected by collectivities

63. Those persons who are cut off from the labour force and remain outside the flow of money distribution in the form of interest on capital present problems of a different nature. Collectivities, and more particularly the State, must look after them and laws must be introduced enabling them to receive the money they need in order to live. No country has so far succeeded altogether in setting up the proper machinery to meet the case, and the persons concerned are, generally speaking, unfairly treated as compared with the other population categories. In most cases this is not due to insufficient production. The goods and services exist in the places where these persons are living, but they do not have the necessary money to pay for them, and the spectacle of unused goods and services in the face of palpable need is one of the most distressing paradoxes at the present time.

The lowering of the death-rate as a result of the progressive disappearance of the endogenous causes of death should soon render the problem so acute that society will be obliged to find solutions.

In exactly the same way as for the procedure based on capital income, doubt-less the distribution of income by collectivities cannot exceed a certain thresh-old. Rightly or wrongly, the worker has the feeling that what he produces belongs to him, and the proportion deducted from such production cannot be indefinitely increased in order to distribute it among those who do not form part of the labour force. It is clear that social demographic data concerning these classes of persons are indispensable for the planner. He must know the number of persons to date in each class and also the rate of increase through the years. Thus one comes up against the need for new perspectives, related this time no longer to consumption rates but to the way in which persons acquire the money they need in order to live. It is not difficult to imagine who those persons are: the aged no longer in employment, widows with children to bring up, orphans, unemployed persons, the sick, 'outsiders', etc. All the demographic history of these groups remains to be studied. How does one begin? and where? How is one to solve the difficulties? It will be the demographer's task in the coming years to discover the laws governing all such phenomena.

Planners must also know what characteristics are likely to induce these persons to become reincorporated in the labour force: desire to remain active, possibility of attending a refresher course, finding a help for the household, undergoing a readaptation course, especially in the case of the disabled, etc. Socio-demographic researches alone can provide the answers to these questions.

The international market

64. There is a special type of money which all countries are very interested in possessing – the type which can be exchanged on the international money market and which countries obtain by means of a variety of international operations (trade, tourism, loans, gifts, etc.).

The goods and services offered to the population of a country are never used to the fullest extent, especially the services. Thus there are often vacant seats in theatres, cinemas, museums, trains, aeroplanes, etc. The economic value of such marginal goods and services is small and they can frequently be offered free of charge. But as soon as a foreign tourist takes advantage of them, they immediately acquire a great value. When a foreign tourist sits down in a cinema in a seat which would otherwise have remained empty, it is just as though the country had an additional worker at its disposal and, what is more, a high quality one at that, since he is free to choose his kind of activity. For with the money spent by the tourist, the country will be able to buy anything it likes on the international market.

Once more, one meets with the three chief means of obtaining money available for use on the international market – labour, capital income, and recourse to foreign States.

The income obtained from labour can be direct when a country has living abroad some of its workers who have not severed their ties with the mother country and send remittances to it. This form of income can be quite large in some cases, but remains small taken as a whole. The amount of income received through international trade is decidely greater: in selling its products, a country is, in effect, selling its work.

Income derived from capital follows exactly the same course as that described at the national level.

Income from foreign States which was for a long time supplied under colonialist conditions is now given more and more in the form of bilateral or international aid.

65. Such means have their limit – and in the first place of a currency order – on an international scale, exactly as they have on a national scale. Whoever possesses currency that can be exchanged on the international market is able to obtain whatever he wants with it. If this power is too widespread, and especially if it is misused, it can endanger the normal working of the international monetary system. We saw this recently in connexion with what was called the gold crisis. Economic aid is naturally limited by the generosity of the donors. In this connexion, the United Nations made the following proposition to the wealthy countries, namely, 1% of their national revenue, which percentage, in the aggregate,[20] has never yet been reached.[21] Income derived from capital is, taken as a whole, restricted to 25% of the total world product.

But this refers to global limitation. Just as, in a given country, the limitation of capital income to 25% of the gross national product does not prevent certain persons from obtaining very big incomes by this means, so there are countries which obtain a great deal of money by lending abroad. There are also countries which receive considerably more economic aid than the average. On the international level, countries play the same rôle as do individuals of a particular country. But whereas there are a great many individuals, there is only a small number of countries, about one hundred, and the exceptions are no longer submerged in the general mass. On the contrary, they stand out as examples and might well be put forward as standard types without it being noticed that, in point of fact, they are exceptional cases.

66. But, it will be said, we have got far away from the subject of demography. I am not so sure. The exchange currencies on the international market often constitute the key to economic development for those countries which possess such currency. When added to the national savings, the total represents the investment potential and determines, in consequence, the rate at which the production growth-plan can be carried out. But, the difference between this production growth-rate and the population growth-rate is a rough measurement of the growth in the standard of living. By a boomerang effect, the growth in the standard of living has an impact on the savings effected and on the development of international trade.

All these factors are connected with each other without our yet knowing in exactly what manner, and yet it is through being aware of such connexions that one might expect to bring about the economic development of the developing countries, thus avoiding the fixing *a priori* of unattainable aims. For instance, if it were found that the suggestion made by the United Nations Organization to the rich countries, whereby each country devoted 1 % of its national revenue yearly to assist the poor countries, was incompatible with the proper functioning of the present international monetary system, then measures for reducing the fertility rate of the poor countries would be of top priority. If, on the other hand, machinery were to be devised enabling transfers from rich countries to poor countries to be increased with impunity, the high population growth-rates in the developing countries could be accepted more easily.

Irreconcilable aims

67. So far, we have considered economic problems from the sole standpoint of the creation of a certain level of production and the distribution to consumers of the necessary currency for obtaining the goods and services produced. However, society has a number of other aims which may often be incompatible with the aim of maximum production. We shall review them briefly.

68. An economic development plan often presents the necessity of ensuring full employment. This matter has not been touched upon so far. With the production of goods and services at the desired level, and the currency-distribution machinery duly functioning, the matter was then regarded as solved, even if only half the potential working population was actually in employment. All that was necessary was that this currency distribution should provide for those not in work. If, in addition, what is wanted is that every one should have employment, everything will have to be reconsidered and it is then not certain whether the economic structure finally arrived at will not entail a decrease in production.

69. The right to education can also be at variance with the aims of production. There is no doubt that by offering too great a number of young people the opportunity to reach the higher branches of education, in the first place their arrival on the labour market is delayed and the number of workers is thereby reduced, but more important still, there is the risk of training a working pop-

ulation ill-adapted to the aims of production. There is the danger that the gap between the working population required for carrying out the plan and the working population receiving a university training will be widened, and we have already shown how this discrepancy was at the bottom of dangerous social tensions. The Human Rights Conference, held in Teheran in 1968, accentuated still further this conflict by laying down the right of each individual to choose freely his own employment.

70. If absolute priority is given to the right to health, that also can render the aims of the production plan unattainable. We have already observed how the increasingly excessive cost of the new forms of medical care is likely to result in a revision of the principle whereby society is in duty bound to do everything possible to protect the health of its members.

71. The right to leisure, or, more precisely, to rest, is of course central to any plan for economic development. There are as a matter of fact two ways to utilize the results of increased productivity: produce more per capita or shorten working hours. Both ways have been used in the past, doubtless without fully realizing that such a choice was involved. There is today a tendency to believe that one can independently set length of leisure time and production goals, leaving it to automation to iron out the difficulties. This is of course a view of the problem fraught with illusions. In fact automation does not decrease the number of jobs, but rather transforms them; and if in the long run one can succeed in increasing at the same time production per capita and the length of leisure time, it must be realized that these are two objectives which can be irreconcilable if one wants to advance too quickly.

72. Finally, there is a right which so far has been looked forward to rather than experienced by the majority of the human race, but which is gradually becoming a reality and constitutes an essential variable in economic and social development, namely, the right to plan one's family.

Short-term fluctuations in the economy
73. Hitherto we have spoken of economic progress as though it were a continuous movement towards a better way of living. But we know, in actual fact, that it is made up of a series of more or less regular jolts, involving improvement on the one hand, followed by losses on the other. As long as fertility remained at the stage described as 'social', very powerful economic fluctuations were needed before their effects were felt on the number of births. But now that the birth of a child is left to the discretion of the parents, all the economic ups and downs consciously experienced, or simply expected or even imagined, are likely to have a decided repercussion on fertility. It is not even a question here of the effects of the fluctuation itself, but of the use which is made of them, and behavioural changes can take place in couples which are quite out of proportion to the economic happening as such. Moreover, boomerang effects are to be expected. Indeed, while economic development exerts pressure on the fertility-

rate, the fluctuations of the latter also have their influence on the economy. Something resembling a perpetual series of oscillations could even result, economy and fertility-rate varying indefinitely, changes in the one giving rise to variations in the other. A whole new behavioural science lies here ready to be created in which sociology, political economy and demography should help each other.

IV. DEMOGRAPHIC RESEARCH AND HUMAN ECOLOGY

74. In order to exercise his functions as a consumer and producer, and to prepare himself for the same, to start a family, have children, make arrangements for his old age, and finally, die, man settles down in his outer environment through a process of mutual adaptation, modifying the environment and at the same time accepting certain aspects of it. Human ecology is the study of these relations between man and his environment.

Migrations

75. We have already referred to the importance of migratory movements, and they traditionally form part of demographic research. The researcher aims at getting to know their scope, direction and motivation, but these aims, it must be admitted, have remained very far ahead of the results so far achieved. We can learn a lot from population censuses about the distribution of population in a given territory and the growth of the various localities, but they tell us nothing about the inner dynamics of such movements. All these localities appear to be the scene of powerful going and coming movements. Annual intake and exit rates of around 40 per 1,000 are by no means uncommon, and the positive or negative balance of 4 to 5 per 1,000 revealed by the census seems to leave out of account the essential aspect of the matter. From the point of view of the inhabitants of a locality, there is not much difference between a situation in which the arrival rate is 40 per 1,000 and the departure rate 30 per 1,000 and the reverse situation: arrival rate 30 per 1,000 and departure rate 40 per 1,000. In each case the locality witnesses the departure of an important section of its inhabitants and has to extend a welcome to about the same number of new arrivals. One can hardly believe that the newcomers take the place of the leavers.

In fact, such movements are invariably accompanied by changes in the demographic, economic, social and cultural structure, and if a town with a surplus of leavers has a little less difficulty in absorbing arrivals than has one with a surplus of arrivals, the two problems do not differ essentially. What can be described as the 'floating population', composed of those who decided to go and of those who came to stay, represents just about the same number in each case.

The importance of such going and coming movements is obvious. That new science concerned with 'the organization of the territory' *(aménagement du territoire)* requires that we should know about them if we want to be able to channel them. Research in this connexion has been begun in a good many places. The processing of data collected by population censuses with the aid of electronic computers ought to help in the development of such studies. In fact, it is now possible to compare information obtained concerning the *same* person in the course of two successive censuses.[22] By joining to this data supplied by registry office records, it is possible to analyse arrival and departure flows. The initial application of this method has produced very promising results.

76. However, the statistical analyses of existing documents are not enough. All they can do is to prepare the way for more exact longitudinal studies showing the effects of migratory movement in a person's life. Here are a few of the questions that have so far remained unanswered. Does the migrant preserve the fertility and life-expectancy rates of his country of origin, and if not, how long does it take him to acquire the habits of his new country of residence? Which are the migrants who return to their own country and under what conditions is this return effected? How is the social, economic, political and cultural integration of non-returning migrants effected? All those preliminaries in order at last to try to answer the basic question: Why does such and such a person leave his homeland while another remains there?

Town-planning

77. The overall (at the national or regional level) point of view of the planner concerned with the greater or lesser population density in a given part of the territory, is something altogether different. Whereas in the immediately preceding paragraphs we were concerned with the development of localities (that is, towns or urban development), here we are dealing with what is called urbanization, which corresponds to something of another order. A country becomes urbanized when the proportion of its inhabitants living in towns goes on increasing. Although the two phenomena generally go together, one could, strictly speaking, have urbanization without urban development. Seeing that the more or less urban nature of localities is bound up with economic and sociocultural characteristics, it is the study of urbanization which throws light on a country's all-round policy in its most varied aspects. Urban development as such is restricted to a particular locality. We can say that while it is the mayor of a locality who studies urban development, it is the government ministers who study the question of a country's urbanization.

78. Very early on, human beings realized that the city was a factor making for cultural development, and it can be said that all or just about all we call 'civilization' derives from the fact that men learned to establish cities. We tend to forget this too easily when we count the disadvantages that have also accompanied this creative achievement. Without wishing in the least to minimize these disadvantages, it must be admitted that the balance is very much on the credit side, and one of the features of the present day is the craze for the urban type of life, which must be regarded as a fact of existence rather than as a reversible parameter. This brings us to the living conditions whose description, understanding and improvement are made possible by the study of urban development.

79. Migratory movements towards the towns have genetic results, the importance of which has not yet been fully appreciated. The most gifted are attracted to the towns and so the country districts slowly lose their best elements. This factor is even beginning to produce an effect at the international level. The brain-drain being carried out by the most economically developed countries is a subject which should enlist the attention of demographers.

80. At the same time, it is an open question whether the tendency to create bigger and bigger urban centres – megapolises, as they are called – will continue at the rate with which we are familiar.

The technical progress about to take place in high-speed mass transport could call into question the existence of such 'megapolises'. As long as man was obliged to move about on foot, the size of towns was limited by his physical walking powers, as it was then impossible to live too far from the place of work. Water, the horse, the railway, and finally the motor-car changed this situation and extended considerably the range of urban centres.[23] Magazines of the beginning of the century have pictures of those later known as suburbanites arriving in the morning at the railway stations to work in the cities. A whole new sociology developed around this new means of transport which contributed enormously to the creation of 'megapolises'. The motor-car, owing to its being an individual means of transport, arrived to upset everything. In multiplying by five the surface transport congestion per person, it has brought cities to the very verge of total paralysis.

The new means of rapid mass transport

81. The new means of rapid mass transport which we are told are about to be realized will perhaps involve a complete overhaul of the situation. We are promised trains on air cushions able to go at three or four hundred km. an hour. One can imagine that it will only need a few years to approach the speed of sound; so it is thinking in terms of mass transport movements at, say, 1,000 km. (6–7 hundred miles) an hour that we have to envisage the situation of our present-day cities. There can be little doubt that no method of individual transport will ever attain such speeds as those. Consequently, mass transport is bound to recover an overwhelming superiority. When it will take only twelve minutes to get to work 125 miles from one's place of residence, the geographical distribution of populations will be based on very different criteria from those of the present day.

At the same time, cities ought to be able to rid themselves of hundreds of thousands of cars which block the streets every morning and evening. This means that the transport services within cities will themselves have to be reorganized. It does not seem too early to try to imagine what urban life could be like based on such technological innovations – for these innovations will be here tomorrow. It is on these bases that the megapolis of the year 2,000 will function. These new means of transport could also affect the use of country homes, since it will be possible to live in them all the year around.

The new audio-visual means of communication

82. In addition to the changes of residence which number perhaps three or four on an average during the life of an individual, and the more or less daily journeys to and fro because people nowadays often live at a distance from their place of work, there is a kind of shifting about occasioned by the particular type of work. For instance, the intellectual has to go to his library, the engineer or business man to consult with professional colleagues, the scientist to take part in conferences, etc.

The progress already achieved or envisaged in transmitting information by what are called audio-visual media should alter the type of such comings and goings and make them less frequent. It is now technically possible, thanks to television, to organize a 'meeting' of industrialists scattered about between, say, New York, Buenos Aires, Sydney, Tokyo, London and Paris without them having to go outside their respective offices. Soon it will be possible to do the same for 200 persons. There seems to be no limit. No doubt such 'meetings' will be considerably lacking in human warmth; but as they will not cost much, it will be possible to hold them far more frequently and engage the most suitable persons to take part in them, so that one thing will balance another.

Another technical invention already brought out, but as yet in little use, is going to upset completely the traditional method whereby one sets out to obtain the information required. It will soon become current practice, without stirring a step, to address an inquiry to a machine and receive the answer at home – and a printed answer at that.

83. Lastly, seasonal migratory movements, whether connected with work or holidays, are becoming ever greater and greater, and will make their effects felt more and more in the social and economic life of a country.

V. DEMOGRAPHIC RESEARCH AND SOCIOLOGY

84. When dealing with human ecology, we were already in the realm of sociology. As Jean Stoetzel has said, 'Ecology is on the borderline between the science of population and that of social phenomena; (it) constitutes the natural bridge between these two branches of knowledge'. Sociology contributes to demography its theories, principles and methods. We give below a few examples of sociological theories serving as a fulcrum for demographic research.

85. On several occasions we have been led to emphasize the voluntary aspect of demographic events: a birth, a marriage, a migration are more and more the result of some individual decision. In the case of a death, there is a mingling of individual decision and collective decision, without it being possible to see very clearly as yet which will prevail. Indeed, there is a branch of sociology exclusively occupied with 'decision'. It discerns in the various circumstances in which a choice is necessary the use of standard procedures which are applicable to demographic events, and this broadening of the notion of choice should help the demographer to understand the variations which he notes in his findings.

86. For the demographer, a fundamental choice is that of the marriage partner, which has obvious genetic, economic and social repercussions. There is something that he finds difficult to describe owing to the fact that he is dealing with two distinct population entities – marriageable men and women among whom motives of attraction and repulsion exist which will decide the composition of the couples, with many other variables added, such as composition according to age, social group, religion, colour, etc. Is it possible to measure such motives of attraction and repulsion? That is a matter for sociological research.

87. There is another field in which sociology can assist the demographer – that of the relations between the generations. In most of the industrialized countries, the birth-rate went up after the second world war. Children born from 1945 onwards have been brought up in a relatively large family circle. They are now reaching the age for having children of their own. It is quite possible that their attitude towards fertility will take the form of a reaction against their own home environment. Hence we can imagine alternate sequences of greater or lesser fertility between generations. However attractive this idea may be, it remains simply a conception of the mind until its truth has been established. But if this reactive behaviour is true, it will not be restricted to fertility: it will be found in the majority of attitudes which go to make up social life. If sociology can demonstrate this, then the demographer will know that the explanation *he* gives must be included within a wider frame of reference altogether. He will likewise know that his idea can be elaborated on and arrange his findings in consequence.

88. The behaviour of an individual in a particular situation is often contradictory, depending on which aspect is being considered. Demographic events are naturally subject to such contradictions. One person will insist, for example, that society must do everything in its power to save the life of a sick man, but will consider the health-insurance contribution to be much too expensive. Another will dream about receiving a good pension on retirement, but will at the same time insist that families should be reduced in size, forgetting that those children which society does not have are going to make their absence felt when it comes to producing what is necessary to supply his retirement needs. We could think of any number of such examples. Are these contradictions so much as recognized by the individuals concerned? And if so, are they regarded as embarrassing for the general purpose of everyday life? These are questions which sociology can answer and the reply given will be of importance to the demographer, for instance, in the research he conducts into ways of influencing demographic development.

89. But sociology has also its standards of judgement to bring to the cause of demography, and more particularly in the use that is made of social stratification. In fact, all the demographer's investigations are stratified and, as a rule, according to the social characteristics of the persons interrogated.

Conversely, however, demographic forms of behaviour differ according to the social group, and demographic development brings about changes in society.

90. To sum up, sociology uses the same methods as demography. The demographer notes, observes and measures phenomena. He unravels the 'how' of things and calls upon the sociologist to help him find the 'wherefore' of them. He discovers, for instance, that matrimonial habits vary from one region to another. In order to do this, he has started off with numerical data supplied to him by the census and civil registry office. Then, in the variations he notices in this data, he takes into account those which are due to factors other than matrimonial habits. He is then able to define and calculate the degree of what he calls the 'marriage situation'. Carrying on with his analysis, he discovers that the 'marriage situation' varies according to social class, profession, education, religion, etc.; that it also varies in time, depending on the economic development, season of the year, etc. But how is he to understand that these are regarded as standard habits by this or that social group? By using the methods of sociology, the demographer is able to show how demographic events take their place within a socio-cultural framework which gives them meaning.

VI. DEMOGRAPHIC RESEARCH AND MEANS OF OBSERVATION

91. In every science, research is also affected by the means of observation. Progress in those means entails progress in every branch of science. For instance, the discovery of optical instruments in physics made research possible in hitherto unsuspected fields. During the past few years, progress in three sectors has been observable in demography and, more generally, in the human sciences as a whole, the effects of which on research are being and will continue to be felt for a long time to come. These are:
a. the development of techniques for collection of sample survey data;
b. the development of techniques for data analysis by demographers and statistical theorists, and
c. the invention of ever more advanced electronic computers.

Sample surveys
92. For many years, demography has drawn most of its source material from official statistical publications, based for the most part on results of population censuses and records in the civil registry. It was for a long time believed that anything and everything could be obtained from such documents. We now know that they have their limitations. The tendency is rather to simplify them and to rely on surveys for the accumulation of more varied information.

However, there is more to it than that: apart from the administrative purposes for which they were created, censuses and civil registration returns have always had, above all, an informative purpose. They are required to increase our knowledge, and that was enough so long as demography confined itself to the description of phenomena. In sample surveys, one observes in order to see, without knowing in advance what is going to be found.[24] We rely on sampling to increase our understanding, and it became indispensable from the moment when demography set itself the task of comprehending phenomena.

Progress in data analysis

93. But it is not only the method of collecting data that has been changed; progress has also been made in analytical methods. Demography has given birth to a new discipline: demographic analysis, which has clarified ideas, classified methods, caused principles to be reviewed, and raised questions. It is in full process of development and ought to make its presence still more felt in the years immediately ahead.

Remarkable progress has also been achieved in mathematical statistics, offering the researcher new methods of analysis.

A certain hesitancy is still observable in putting these new methods to use, because they call for detailed calculations the results of which cannot be foreseen.

Electronic computers

94. Electronic computers ought to get rid of this disadvantage. One might hesitate when faced with a calculation requiring several weeks' work. There is no longer any need for this when the same calculation can be done electronically in a few seconds. This means, it is true, that the researcher should have been trained accordingly, and no doubt training programmes should now be altered to take this new development into account.

95. But demography stands to gain even more from electronic computing. Like most of the human sciences, demography is unable to make use of experiment to which researchers in the natural sciences owe their most brilliant discoveries. Besides, we have already explained how the observer disturbs phenomena by the mere fact of observing them. For the human sciences, these are serious handicaps. However, electronic computing, by making it possible to simulate the behaviour of populations, is in the process of rapidly changing the situation. By making use of the laws of probability in their effect on individual motivations established by correct analysis of an observation of demographic events, it is possible in an electronic computer to simulate the result of the adoption of such laws by a population. And by causing these laws to vary, the conditions for a pseudo-experiment are brought about. One can, in particular, observe the variation in phenomena by repeating the experiments. Up to now, we did not know how to *calculate* this variation except in very simple cases, as the formulas quickly became extremely complicated. Although it is useful to know the average value of a parameter, it is often equally useful to know how that parameter is distributed about such an average. Indeed, it is indispensable if the object is to compare a number of populations with each other.

It is not yet very clear where this use of simulations on electronic machines is going to lead us, but we may expect it to prove of very considerable aid to demographic research, so long as it is not forgotten that nothing will ever be able to replace direct observation of reality. The appearance of new methods of analysis and of electronic computers has not only influenced research, but has also had an effect on the teaching of demography: today demographers must receive substantial training in mathematics.

96. The application of population policies offers a good illustration of the difficulties encountered experimentally. For instance, in order to facilitate family planning, the question of which contraceptive measures were best suited to a given cultural environment was considered. Several groups of couples were formed to whom different sorts of contraceptives were given, and the results were observed. In this way, the necessary conditions for a proper experiment were established. Unfortunately, individuals in one group very quickly discovered that those in another group had different contraceptive means from theirs and this led to various exchanges. Reactions on the part of the observed thus had a disturbing effect on the conditions for the experiment.

It has sometimes been thought that when a government brought in legislation concerning family allowances it was engaged in a genuine experiment, but it cannot revert to the preceding situation. If it finds it has made a mistake, it is unable to rectify it, and it sets in motion an evolution rather than an experiment.

97. In contrast to the special lines of research which we have indicated above, and which were connected with specific problems, we must henceforth expect research to be developed in every direction as a result of the progress made in the means of observation.

VII. THE CONTRIBUTION OF DEMOGRAPHIC RESEARCH TO THE OTHER SCIENCES

98. Every time a branch of science helps to solve a question raised by demographic research, it stands to benefit itself from the research work thus instigated. So we can say that with regard to each of the subjects we have examined, demographic research has some contribution to make to the sciences concerned.

99. Just as demographic research, however, finds itself held up by unsolved questions in the other sciences, so it is likely that these same sciences also encounter matters that have not yet been studied by the demographer, because he is for the most part unaware of those sectors to which his research could be directed so as to be of use to others.

Hence the demographer is badly placed for indicating in what way he can help in the development of the other sciences. This is rather the task of specialists in the other sciences. We shall therefore confine ourselves to a few general considerations.

100. The term 'population' has a very general sense. Its use is often limited to human populations. But the statistician employs it for any group of objects. Among all these 'populations', he distinguishes those which renew themselves by a process of arrivals and departures. This is the case with human populations, but there are many others besides, such as animal populations. We can also refer to vegetation populations – for instance a forest – and to microbial populations. We can even talk of populations of objects: a series of types of electric light bulbs is a well-known example; the books in a library is another. The methods used by the demographer for studying the evolution of human populations can be applied to other sorts of population. But we must all the same take care when analytical methods are thus extended. Certain peculiarities attached to human populations are connected with the form of the fertility and mortality functions of the human species. When populations other than human populations are considered, the arrival and departure functions will, as a rule, be different from such fertility and mortality functions. It would be extremely useful, therefore, if the demographer could distinguish very clearly in his studies between, on the one hand, what is true for all self-renewing populations, and on the other hand, what is true only for human populations.

101. We remarked at the beginning of this chapter how one of the essential characteristics of demographic events was that of being events as part of history. This characteristic is not peculiar to demographic events. It is found in all the human sciences, but in the case of demography, it lies at the very core of the matter and cannot be eluded. All phenomena which form part of an historical process share this common characteristic, namely, that they unfold in successive stages in such a way that it is impossible for them to reach a given stage without having gone through all the preceding stages. A whole method of analysis has been built round this characteristic. There are, however, many phenomena unconnected with demography to which the same analysis can be applied. We mention, for example, the circulation of products in a market economy; the circulation of vehicular traffic from place to place; the building of a succession of barrages along a river; the tax on increased nominal value, etc. – all subjects in which the demographer can collaborate.

102. We have a recent example of the results to be derived from such collaboration, namely research into historical demography. In many countries, long before the establishment of a civil registration system, marriages, births and deaths were registered by the religious authorities in what are called in Europe parish registers. These documents, which are very numerous, had not, until quite recently, been systematically used. Demographers have found means for dealing with them and have applied those means with such success that they are now used by historians.[25]

103. The human being has remarkable powers of adaptation, but these should not be developed too rapidly. If environmental conditions change too quickly they give rise to tensions which can endanger the very existence of the social

body. The increasing speed of technological progress which we are witnessing is the cause of such a phenomenon. As a result of this acceleration, within ten years the training received will no longer correspond to the level reached by technology. Consequently in industrialized countries there are increasing numbers of workers insufficiently equipped for their task. A study of the characteristics of this section of the population in difficulties ought to help towards reinstating it in the economic and social circuit.

104. The same is true, moreover, of a number of other sections of the population, such as the unemployed, those on the sick-list, etc.

105. Politics is another field which stands to benefit from the progress in demographic research. Numerous decisions of a political nature have demographic consequences which call for the use of methods of demographic analysis in order to be understood and which, therefore, only demographers are in a position to interpret accurately.

106. Political science itself has often had recourse to demographic data as a foundation for its doctrines. The best known case is that of Malthus at the end of the eighteenth century, but there have been more recent examples. Such doctrines require the assistance of demographers for taking the consequences of the principles on which they are based to their ultimate conclusions.

VIII. ORGANIZATION OF DEMOGRAPHIC RESEARCH

The three requisites for an organization of research
107. The success of research depends very much on the surroundings in which it takes place. To have a research programme is not enough; it must be carried out.

To begin with, all research requires a body providing the researcher with the necessary means. In its most elaborate form this will be, for example, a specialized institute which will offer the researcher the necessary room-space and equipment to enable him to work, see to the collection and distribution of financial resources, and, lastly, sanction expenditure. In its simplest form, this would be, for instance, a grant of funds for carrying out a given piece of research. Between these two extremes, a number of other situations are readily conceivable.

108. In view of the fact that demographic research relates to many different branches of science, an institute, by gathering together under the same roof researchers from different branches, obviously provides a co-operative element which is absent when research is conducted individually, and from this point of view there is much to be gained by making an institute's range of interest as wide as possible.

109. In addition, the researcher needs to submit his findings to the scrutiny of his colleagues. Research is a collective enterprise in which each researcher draws sustenance from the work of others similarly engaged. It is important for *him* that the results of his work should be discussed, or even criticized. This can be done in writing, in which case the journal, printed report or even book is the means employed. But if it is by word of mouth, we then have the symposium, conference, congress, or seminar, etc. We should add that teaching also quite often takes a share in both forms of expression. A scientific course, occasionally printed, provides an opportunity for setting forth the results of research.

110. And this brings us to the third requirement of research: it needs researchers. In each branch of science, therefore, it is necessary to arrange for a form of instruction which can either be incorporated in instruction as a whole, or else be given in specialized schools.

Need for international co-operation
111. The organization of research as we have just described it is the type that is usually found at the national level. In the first place, questions of language limit the geographical scope, and secondly, the source of funds – in most cases national – produces the same effect. That is why international contacts between scientists working in the same branch need to be organized. This is the object of private international associations which undertake to arrange meetings, publish journals, or even entire works.

112. It often happens that research passes beyond the scope of a single country. For instance, the expense involved may be too heavy for it. It is also possible that the research is of a supra-national interest, making co-operation between several countries necessary. In such cases as these, governmental or private international institutions have their part to play.

Practical applications on a national scale
113. Let us now see how these principles have been applied in the organization of demographic research. Here, we must have a little look at history. To start with, emphasis was placed on research institutes and the teaching side was neglected. After using for a long time the data from population censuses and civil registration statistics as its only source of raw material, demographic research, on its first appearance, naturally found its field of operation in the official statistical services of the various countries. This situation continued up to the first world war. After the war, various institutes made their appearance, but for a long time they never exceeded ten in number. These were:
in the United States:
— the Scripps Foundation for Research in Population Problems, founded in 1922 at Miami University (Ohio);
— the Office of Population Research, founded in 1936 at Princeton University (New Jersey);

— the Milbank Memorial Fund, a private institution founded in New York immediately after the first world war;
— the Population Research and Training Center, founded in 1947 at Chicago University (Illinois).

in France:
— the Institut national d'études démographiques, founded in 1945, in Paris, as a research institute coming under the Ministry of Social Affairs.

in Japan:
— the Institute of Population Problems, founded in 1939 in Tokyo, and attached to the Ministry of Health.

in Italy:
— the Comitato Italiano per lo Studio dei Problemi della Popolazione, founded in Rome in 1928.

in Brazil:
— the Laboratório de Estatística, established in Rio de Janeiro immediately following on the 1940 census, and forming part of the Instituto Brasileiro de Geografia e Estatística.

in the United Kingdom:
— the Population Investigation Committee, established in 1936 in London.

in Spain:
— the Instituto Balmes de Sociología y Asociación para el Estudio Científico de los Problemas de Población, research institute founded in 1943.

All these organizations founded between 1922 and 1947 were originally interested essentially in research. Many of them very soon began to publish technical reviews, and all of them have published reports and other works setting forth the results of their researches.

114. At the international level, co-operation between demographers first began to develop through the International Statistical Institute (I.S.I.) founded in 1885; then in 1928 demographers grouped themselves together in the International Union for the Scientific Study of Population (I.U.S.S.P.). Finally, the Biometric Society was established in 1944. At the meetings of the I.S.I. and during the conferences held by the I.U.S.S.P. and the Biometric Society, demographers have been able to exchange their points of view.

115. The above-mentioned institutes, with their publications, and the three international associations that have just been mentioned, with their conferences, fulfilled the first two requisites for enabling research to go forward. Nevertheless, these various institutions differed considerably from one another both as regards their size and the scope attributed to demography. The creative spirit produced by the juxtaposition of researchers from different disciplines was often lacking. All had the disadvantage of not taking sufficient interest in the teaching of demography. To remedy this situation, either developing this teaching within the institutions themselves or its separate autonomous development could be considered. In fact, both courses were adopted.

116. In the United States, for example, although the Scripps Foundation[26] and the Milbank Memorial Fund have remained research institutes, the other institutes have developed their educational activities. Moreover, within the last twenty years, numerous other centres have been founded which immediately combined teaching with research. In France, teaching and research have tended to follow separate paths. University institutes have been created, notably the Institut de démographie of the University of Paris (i.d.u.p.). In addition, the teaching of demography has been made compulsory in certain branches of general teaching. As a result these two countries have fulfilled all the necessary conditions for the development of demographic research, and it is not by accident that they are now the ones where this type of research is most actively pursued. On the other hand, in Japan and Brazil which have kept their research institutes as they were, without reserving even the smallest place to teaching, no progress has been made in demographic research.

117. Let us mention yet another recent example – the creation in 1963, in Budapest, of the Research Group for Population Studies (now the Demographic Research Institute). Shortly afterwards, the first number of the review published by the Group appeared, giving the results of work undertaken by researchers. In 1964, the Group organized an international symposium on social mobility and fertility, followed by a second one in 1965. At the same time, exchanges of researchers with those of other countries were arranged. We observe again the various steps taken in the organization of research. But we also find the same flaw – no provision for teaching. However, this has just been remedied. Since 1967 courses in demography have been given by researchers belonging to the Group at the University of Budapest.

118. Along with the successes, it is interesting to observe, if not exactly the failures, at any rate the attempts that have not led to any notable results. Such is the case with Germany and Italy. In these two countries, demographic research was organized in the thirties under the national statistical services. That was a bad beginning in view of the priority given by those services to short-term affairs. For since demographic factors follow a slow process of development and do not make their presence immediately felt, they were bound to be neglected sooner or later. But that is not all. The successful demographic researches carried out in those two countries at that time were due to the powerful personalities of the men conducting them, whose failing was to place their branch of science at the service of politics. The collapse of the political systems so served brought about their disappearance from the international demographic scene. To this day, the Italian – and especially the German – demographers have been unable to surmount this crisis.[27] So it would seem that demography's own independent research with respect to the other branches of science – in this case statistics – and with respect to the public authorities is all-important.

Practical applications on an international scale
119. We now come to the rôle of the international governmental organizations.

We have already said how, for a long time, censuses and civil registers were the essential sources for data on which demographers had to base their work. In those days, it was only the variety of national conditions which gave the researcher the appearance of conducting experiments. Hence it was essential to reach a certain homogeneity in the information collected by the various countries. The International Statistical Institute originally undertook to encourage international co-operation in this field, but a private institution such as this lacked the powers possessed by the international governmental organizations, and so the United Nations Organization was given the task of standardizing questionnaires, methods of collecting data, and tabulation procedures.[28] All it amounts to really is preparatory work for research purposes, but of essential importance in itself; the Statistics Committee of the Economic and Social Council issues the directives, and these are carried out by the Bureau of Statistics of the United Nations.

120. Among the aims of the United Nations Organization, the economic and social development of the developing countries was very quickly given a high priority, and in the efforts made to further this development the demographic obstacle became immediately apparent. It was also found that the mutual relationships between population growth and the economic and social development aimed at were not properly known. Accordingly, demographic research became of supra-national importance, and there was room for international action. This action has been developed by following lines of approach similar to those followed by individual countries, viz:

a. Founding regional institutes for teaching and research: one for Latin America, one for Asia and the Far East, and one for Africa.
b. Publishing of reports and textbooks.
c. Organizing courses of professional studies and convening world and regional conferences.

The Population Committee of the Economic and Social Council draws up the programmes which are carried out by the Population Division of the United Nations Secretariat.

An unsolved difficulty
121. The multidisciplinary character of demographic research has been the cause of a difficulty which is far from being overcome.

The large United Nations system is itself multidisciplinary. In addition to the central organization in New York, we have
in Geneva:
— the International Labour Office (ILO), and
— the World Health Organization (WHO);
in Rome:
— the Food and Agriculture Organization (FAO):
in Paris:
— the United Nations Educational, Scientific and Cultural Organization (UNESCO).[29]

In addition there are now four regional economic commissions — for Europe, Asia and the Far East, Latin America and Africa.

This multidisciplinarity, however, goes hand in hand with a dividing-up of responsibilities. Each of the agencies mentioned has its own budget, conferences and programme. The large United Nations system thus creates conditions which are contrary to those necessary for the proper functioning of a research institute where research workers with varied training and interests work together.

This difficulty is now recognized by the United Nations which is considering the establishment of a co-ordinating body. This body will doubtless merely discover that everything is of interest to everybody, and will be hard put to it to allot the part each should take.

It might well be that the establishment of an organization specializing in population questions would meet the difficulties raised by this proposed co-ordination.

The recent creation by the Secretary-General of the United Nations of a special fund for demographic questions is a step, albeit a timid one, in the right direction.

The Advisory Committee on the Application of Science and Technology to Development,[30] a newcomer in the field of population problems, has correctly attacked the issue. At its 10th session held in Vienna (Austria) in December, 1968, it requested the various agencies of the United Nations to present a report on their activities in the field of demography which will be subsequently examined at its 12th session at the end of 1969. The Committee proposes at that time to 'give special attention to the possible need, within the United Nations family, for some new machinery, or a change in existing machinery, to maintain an overall view of the scientific and technological aspects of population problems and policies'.

A special case: the Council of Europe
122. Apart from the United Nations institutions, a number of other international governmental organizations are interested in demographic questions.

There is:
in Paris:
— Organization for Economic Co-operation and Development (OECD);
in Geneva:
— the Intergovernmental Committee for European Migration (ICEM);
in Strasbourg:
— the Council of Europe.

This last organization deserves particular mention. It is the only one having a political arm for translating into action the resolutions adopted by its assembly. This provides an excellent means of encouraging research not possessed by the United Nations Organization which has little authority over governments, and whose appeals in favour of a co-ordinated development of demographic research[31] have so far remained without much effect.

Much can be expected from the experiment now being undertaken by the Council of Europe. In 1966, this body convened a European Demographic

Conference which outlined a plan for a vast research programme. Following on this conference, a committee of experts was, in 1967, given the task of selecting a small number from among the most important subjects for investigation, and these were handed over by the Committee of Ministers of the Council to some ten demographers who were instructed to promote the necessary research in the European research organizations. The action of these demographers will be supported by the authority of 17 governments, members of the Council of Europe, and it is to be hoped that this action will prove more effective than the resolutions passed by the United Nations institutions, which governments, unfortunately, tend too often to ignore.

Finally, in 1971 the Council of Europe is to convene a second European Demographic Conference at which the results of researches thus undertaken will be discussed.

Private initiatives taken
123. We must not forget to mention the activities of private organizations which have greatly contributed towards the progress of demographic research throughout the world. In most cases they are American foundations which do not themselves engage in research, but give financial assistance to individual researchers or to research institutes. Being more flexible than the official organizations, they can intervene precisely in those cases where the latter fail to act, and so they have a far-reaching catalytic effect. We may mention the following:
— the Population Council
— the Ford Foundation
— the Milbank Memorial Fund
— the Carnegie Endowment for International Peace
— the Tata Institute of Social Sciences
— the Getúlio Vargas Foundation

Gaps to be filled
124. Despite the progress made in the last fifty years, the organization of demographic research still appears incomplete. Though its principles seem to have been accepted by all, they are far from being applied everywhere, more often than not because of lack of funds. Teaching, moreover, needs to be co-ordinated between the various countries and, indeed, between the various universities inside these countries. Sound research requires that researchers should receive as uniform a training as possible. We have already pointed out how considerable efforts have been made in the past few years to build a properly equipped educational structure with its professorships, university degrees and textbooks. A good deal remains to be done, and this presents a good opportunity for international action.

125. Lastly, we come to the question of collaboration with scientists of other branches. Collaboration within the limits of the same institute does not solve it entirely, owing to the fact that you cannot assemble together under one roof *all* the scientists whose services will only be needed *now and again*.

IX. SURVEY OF THE PRESENT SITUATION

126. To what extent do demographic researches in progress already foreshadow
the trends mentioned above? That is what we propose to discuss now. We will
obviously not try to draw up a complete list of demographic researches in the
world today. That would be a formidable task. Ten years ago, it was undertaken
and brought to a successful conclusion by the Population Research and Training Center of Chicago University. A voluminous work consisting of nearly 900
pages was compiled by a team of thirty or so demographers belonging to a
number of countries. The first edition was published in 1959 and the last (4th)
in 1964. More recently, two French researchers were commissioned by the
Maison des sciences de l'homme to write a report on present trends in, and
organization of, demographic research for the period 1955–1965. This work was
published in 1966. It covers the researches undertaken during that period in the
form of bibliographical analyses.

Our purpose is quite different: we shall try to pick out the main centres of
interest that are gradually becoming apparent in demographic work.

Health questions

127. In the first place, we find a whole series of activities centred around health
questions. In these, the World Health Organization (WHO) is playing an important pioneering part. Realizing that the living habits of a sick person may be of
more significance in the determination of his illness than is the specific agent
usually regarded as the causes of it, the General Assembly of WHO approved the
establishment within the organization of a special service to promote research
aimed at a rethinking of the very concept of 'health'. This service, 'by using the
latest advances in modern technology and by constituting a multidisciplinary
group of sophisticated research scientists, including epidemiologists, ecologists,
sociologists, operational research specialists, mathematicians, computer
technologists and others, [hopes] to develop a facility that will be able to predict
the probable developments in a given country in the coming years, which will
enable that country to institute such preventive measures as are possible before
the apparently unavoidable and undesirable side-effects of socio-economic
development and cultural change have had an unalterable effect...'.[32]

128. This international endeavour to introduce the human sciences into the
sphere of medical science has found an echo in a number of countries.

In the United States, a private foundation such as the Milbank Memorial
Fund, considering that in dealing with the problem of public health we are
nowadays faced with a 'maze of social, cultural and economic considerations
which up to now were not the concern of public health authorities', has decided
that it was its duty 'to help to create clusters of trained and even inspired people
who will not apply slavishly the traditional solutions, but who will seek through
innovation and experiment for new ways through the maze.'[33]

Several of the annual conferences organized by the Milbank Memorial Fund
have been devoted to health problems in the modern world.

129. Again in the United States, the studies undertaken by the National Center for Health Statistics, and in particular those based on data collected since 1956 by the National Health Survey through repeated sample surveys on disease and mortality rates in the population, are on similar lines.

130. In the International Biological Programme (IBP), which was established jointly in 1966 by 44 nations and is to continue for a period of ten years, provision is made for a section on man's adaptability to his environment, which will also be dealing with the same problems.

131. This idea that, to arrive at an understanding of a person's 'state of health', it is necessary to take into consideration the whole of his past life, has led to the development of research on differential mortality according to social environment.

The various statistical services in the United Kingdom have for a long time calculated mortality figures according to social class. These figures are difficult to calculate because they represent a relation, in the case of the numerator, to data on mortality (that is to say, data supplied by the statistics on population trends) and, in the case of the denominator, to data supplied by the census. The factor common to both numerator and denominator is the social class, and this factor is therefore determined by reference to different statistical documents. This is bound to result in a lack of homogeneity which falsifies the results. In the United Kingdom, this difficulty is overcome, thanks to the high quality of the demographic statistics. But the same does not apply elsewhere and other methods have recently been devised.

132. The Population Research and Training Center of Chicago University, in co-operation with the national service concerned with population trends and the United States Census Bureau, compared the death certificates of 340,000 persons who died during the four months (May–August) immediately following the census of April 1960 with the census returns for those deceased persons. It was thus possible to determine the 'social class' factor from the census report alone.

Over the past fifteen years, a similar method has been used in France for calculating the infant mortality rate in the various social classes. The death certificates of the children are compared with their birth certificates.

133. Another method used in France for calculating the adult mortality rate consists in keeping a record over the years of a sample group of persons drawn from a population census. This makes it possible to calculate mortality rates according to generation.

134. Mention may also be made of a biometrical survey in Hungary, on a sample of 720 persons chosen from among the candidates in the year 1966 for the university or professional colleges, undertaken by the Research Group for Population Studies of Budapest. The object of this survey is to follow the per-

sons concerned during their educational careers. It therefore goes far beyond a mere study of mortality incidence; on the other hand, it is confined to a particular group of social classes and covers only a short phase of a lifetime.

135. In addition, there are the studies conducted in the United States by the Metropolitan Life Insurance Company on its clientèle. Although not representative of the American population as a whole, this clientèle, consisting of several tens of millions of persons, enables the company to study the influence on the death-rate of factors connected with the way of living. Research is also carried out on morbidity.

136. Rapid progress is being made, too, in research on mortality of genetic origin. There are frequent discoveries of chromosomal disorders responsible for various physiological ailments. It has been demonstrated that the frequency of chromosomal disorders in new-born children is 4 per 1,000, and that chromosomal anomalies account for 20% of the root cause of miscarriages.

137. The question of parental incompatibilities between blood groups raises a number of problems at the present time from the point of view of selection. We are well acquainted with the problem of Rh incompatibilities (hemolytic disease in new-born children), but it is thought that they are to be found also in the ABO and MN systems, among others, with very different mechanisms: gametic selection, selection *in utero*, mortinatality, post-natal selection, specific mortality. All these aspects are of great importance from the point of view of public health.

Procreation in the human race

138. Works on the subject of procreation in the human race relate to another equally important field of research. Three main sectors may be distinguished:

First, the study of the biological and physiological aspects of human reproduction. Here again, we find a vast programme of research launched by WHO. A service specialized in the reproduction of the human species was established in 1965 at the Organization's headquarters in Geneva. It has carried out the following work:

a. It has organized a number of meetings of experts with the object of reviewing the present state of our knowledge and indicating new lines of research. The conclusions of these discussions have been published in the series of technical reports issued by WHO. The mere mention of their titles is enough to show how they fit into the general scheme of this chapter: biology of reproduction (1963),[34] physiology of breast-feeding (1963), effects of confinement on the foetus and new-born child (1964), neuro-endocrinology and the reproduction of the human species (1964), mechanisms of action of sexual hormones and allied substances (1964), biochemistry and microbiology of the genital organs of man and woman (1965), immunization of human reproduction (1965), chemistry and physiology of oral contraceptives and their clinical aspects (1965), gametes (1965), the sterilet and its clinical aspects (1966).

b. It has drawn up a list of research institutes and individual researchers working on the problems of human reproduction.

c. It has encouraged and co-ordinated biological research undertaken in most parts of the world concerning human reproduction, more especially by providing financial aid for laboratory research or surveys. Funds have also been used for the training of technicians.

The service contemplates increasing its activities in the foregoing sectors. It proposes in particular to study the variations, associated with the environmental conditions, to be found in phenomena such as puberty, the menopause, single ovulation, multiple ovulation, anovular cycles, etc. It also proposes to undertake longitudinal studies of genetic histories by trying to discover the effects, on production, of the mother's age, the number of children, the intervals between births, miscarriages, the father's age, the parents' health, the children's health, etc.

139. These same problems are being tackled by demographers, but in this case in relation to populations. Innumerable research projects are in progress; most countries have researchers in this field. They are trying to bring to light the demographic effects of the factors studied in the above-mentioned technical reports of WHO, either through direct observation of present-day populations, or by constructing models, or again through observation of populations of the past, making use of historical documents hitherto unused. Mention may be made of the works of Indian, American, French, Hungarian and British demographers, among others. The limits of such researches have been apparent for some time. To enable them to progress, it is necessary that biology should provide an answer to the questions they raise. The importance of the programme launched by WHO is, therefore, obvious.

140. Another considerable amount of research centred on procreation in the human species is constituted by study of the motivations which determine the size of families.

Over the past ten years or so, sample surveys of couples have been conducted in most parts of the world with the object of discovering the social, economic and psychological reasons for such decisions.

About a hundred of these surveys have taken place, ranging from simple opinion research of the kind carried out in France – this means quota sampling, the conception, execution and analysis of which can be completed in a few months, thus allowing for its repetition – to longitudinal surveys such as the American ones. These involve long-term studies aimed at following a sample of couples over a period of time with the object of recording any changes that may take place in their opinions and attitudes.

These surveys have hitherto been organized without very much co-ordination between them, which has made it difficult to compare the results. The International Union for the Scientific Study of Population has set up a working group to prepare a basic questionnaire for use in all such surveys.

141. The third sector of research relating to human procreation covers everything that has a bearing on birth control.

People did not wait to be thoroughly acquainted with the biological and physiological mechanisms of conception, or with the social, economic and psychological motivations of the founding of a family, before passing on to the practical applications of birth control. Incidentally, biology and physiology come into play again here with the research aimed at discovering contraceptives that are increasingly effective and increasingly easy to use.

Here, the Americans undoubtedly take the lead, and mention should be made of the work done by the National Committee on Maternal Health. Experiments now in progress would seem to indicate the possibility in the near future of ensuring, by means of a single injection, the temporary sterility of a woman for an unlimited length of time that can be chosen at will and in advance.

A whole series of surveys of couples has also been undertaken concerning acceptance of contraceptive practices: acceptance in principle, choice of methods, distribution of information, etc.

Lastly, in all countries that have adopted an active birth control policy, the effects of this policy need to be closely followed, and a methodology for assessing these effects is gradually being evolved.

Economic development

142. A third topic around which several lines of research can be grouped is the relationship between population trends and economic and social development.

A first series concerns the problems raised by the developing countries. A recent work produced by G. Myrdal with the help of several associates[35] gives a remarkable account of research in progress. Information is also to be found in United Nations publications, and more particularly in the work entitled *Determinants and Consequences of Population Trends*, which summed up the state of our knowledge some fifteen years ago and is now being revised. In the past, similar researches were conducted in France and led to the publication of a work on the developing countries. They have lately been resumed and a new work on the developing countries is soon to be published. In these various works, problems have been approached from the macro-economic angle. More or less complicated models have been elaborated, in which the population variable is set beside the economic variables.

143. Another series of researches is centred round the preparation of forecasts of the active population. In this case, the population is no longer considered as a whole; a distinction is drawn between the different sectors of activity and professions.

In outlining the kind of collaboration that might be established between economists and demographers, it was shown that the assistance which could be provided by the latter was mainly in the form of projections: producer and consumer projections (individuals, households, towns, villages, etc.); projections according to the mode of living (urban, rural); projections according to situation in the labour force (retired persons, widows, etc.).

Let us take the case of the preparation of a projection of the active population in relation to a production plan. The demographer can, of course, extrapolate curves of activity rates and calculate the labour force available, on the basis of a population projection according to sex and age. This method is perhaps acceptable from the global standpoint; but it is no longer so when we come to the different branches of economic activity. For some years past, the economists have been drawing up tables showing the exchanges between different branches in terms of monetary units. As long as these same tables are not drawn up in terms of working hours, it will be impossible to know what the production of an extra ton of steel, for example, implies for the active population. Account must also be taken of variations in productivity. Research in this direction, particularly in France, is in its infancy.

144. The methods used in preparing a projection of the active population in relation to a given training are even less precise. We are only just beginning to study this connexion between training and economic activity (France, United Kingdom, United States of America, Federal Republic of Germany, Mexico). The achievement of definite results in this respect is becoming a matter of urgency. It is to be feared that a considerable discrepancy will be found between the active population in relation to training received and the active population in relation to the needs of production. This may well be the root cause of the 'revolt' of the younger generation that we are witnessing in almost all parts of the world.

In the United Kingdom, following the issue of the Robbins report on the shortage of highly qualified personnel, a special research group of the London School of Economics[36] carried out a survey on the factors of work production in the electrical construction industry.

In the United States, the Bureau of Labor Statistics has calculated employment forecasts for 1975, taking account, in particular, of the technological advances to be expected in the coming years and using the double-entry table showing the active population distributed according to occupation and branch of economic activity (known as the 'employment matrix'). A team from the Population Research Center of the University of Pennsylvania in Philadelphia is also working on the subject. Boston's Northeastern University has published a work giving the same employment matrix in respect of some twenty developed countries.

In France, the employment matrix has been used for preparing projections of the active population by occupation. Similar projections have been prepared in Japan.

In the Federal Republic of Germany, similar studies are being carried out by the Institut für empirische Soziologie at Nuremberg.

In the Union of Soviet Socialist Republics, the planning of education is one of the chief factors in economic development plans, though the employment matrix does not seem to be used in this connexion. Apparently, projections relating to skilled workers and middle- and higher-grade personnel are based merely on a detailed analysis of the expected posts in production development.

This is a method of dealing with these problems which is also used in France.

In Mexico, the Centro de Estudios Económicos y Demográficos was established in 1964 by the Colegio de México, and since 1967 it has been publishing a periodical, *Demografía y Economía*. This juxtaposition of the words 'Demografía' and 'Economía' is in itself significant. It shows that there is a real desire to see economists and demographers working together. In the first numbers, interest has been focused on the geographical distribution of the population in relation to economic and regional development.

Projections of the active population have been prepared, taking account of internal migrations. In these studies the macroscopic approach has been adopted, and they should rather be classified among the first series mentioned above. But they are the precursors of other researches that are, moreover, already under way and are following the tradition of the British, American and French studies to which reference has just been made. The Centre intends 'to examine the relations between the economic trend and education'. A pilot project has already been carried out on the relations between higher education, science and technology, on the one hand, and economic development in Mexico, on the other.

Mention should also be made of the work done by OECD (Organization for Economic Co-operation and Development). This organization has tackled the same problems, adopting a different approach. A calculation has been made of the correlations existing between the employment 'structure and a host of indicators of economic production. It is hoped in this way to go on from a plan for the development of production to a projection of employment. The work is proceeding.

OECD has published a methodological work on Argentina, in which it is shown how far it is possible to go by using the traditional methods, that is to say, without making use of the employment matrix.

145. With regard to the active population representing the satisfaction of desires that are universally regarded as legitimate, it has never been calculated, for the same reason for which exchanges between branches are seldom expressed in terms of men. Yet the results would, without any doubt, be highly instructive. We should find that, to satisfy the needs of a population of 50 million, 70 million persons would, for instance, be necessary.[37] This would bring out clearly the absurdity of endeavouring to satisfy all the needs immediately. It would at the same time make it possible to estimate the tensions produced by discrepancies of this type, which explain how it is that the dissatisfaction of the younger generation finds a favourable echo among the rest of the population.

It is doubtful whether such questions can be solved without adopting the principle of shock-teams mentioned earlier in connexion with the Milbank Memorial Fund projects for mortality studies.

146. So far, we have been concerned with producers. In the case of consumers, the problem is easier, since the various categories of consumers are mostly determined with the aid of demographic parameters such as age, civil status,

size of family, rural or urban environment, etc. In most cases, therefore, the calculations are purely a matter for demographers. But this does not solve all the difficulties. For instance, no satisfactory method has yet been devised for preparing projections relating to households or families, and still less so if the number of children has to be taken into account. The Population Division of the United Nations has undertaken to promote research in this matter. It has itself conducted research on urbanization.

147. In the case of populations defined according to the position of individuals in the labour force, research bears principally on three main categories: old people, young people attending school or joining the active population, migrants and their families. A good deal of such research is taking place in most parts of the world. As regards migrations, a team from the Population Center of the University of Pennsylvania (USA) is about to publish a textbook on methods for measuring migratory currents.

148. In all this research centred on economic and social development, the Population Division of the UN, with assistance from UNESCO, ILO and the regional Economic Commissions, could play a pioneering rôle somewhat similar to that which WHO has begun to play in the study of fertility and mortality rates. In which case, its human and financial resources would then have to be increased, since its present activities are more and more taken up with problems connected with birth-control in the developing countries.

Some progress has, moreover, been made recently in this direction. The Population Division of the UN intends to convene, in 1969, a group of experts to advise on the demographic aspects of social development. A textbook on methods of establishing a projection of the active population is to appear in 1968. Studies are in progress concerning urban and rural population forecasts. As regards projections based on occupation, the Population Commission, at its 14th session, in October 1967, stated as follows:

'The future distribution of the population by educational attainment is obviously correlated to the future occupational pattern, and it will be useful for this purpose, therefore, to study the educational and training requirements of workers belonging to different occupations.'

With regard to projections relating to households and families, the Population Commission, at the same session, pointed out 'the need for future analytic work to provide a sound basis for projections relating to households and families, including the investigation of factors influencing formation, growth and dissolution of families and households.'

The importance of these problems and the urgent need for their solution is therefore clearly recognized, but the organization which would be prepared to act as a catalysing agent in the service of all interested parties has not yet been chosen.

Historical demography
149. In the last few years, a series of studies possessing a common characteristic – that of taking their raw material from the past – has contributed towards

developing a new aspect of demography, namely, historical demography. In France, a historical demography society was established in 1962, and publishes yearly records on the subject. In 1967, a research team specializing in the study of the history of the French population was formed, with the help of various research agencies and of the universities.

150. In the United States, the team of graduates and researchers at Harvard University responsible for the periodical *Daedalus* (Journal of the American Academy of Arts and Sciences) organized two international meetings on historical demography, one in Boston (USA) in 1966 and the other in Bellagio (Italy) in 1967.

151. In 1965, a national symposium on historical demography was held in Budapest.

Lastly, a number of research workers belonging to various research institutes now have programmes bearing on the study of populations of the past.

152. So much for the tools. Everything is at hand for a balanced development of the new discipline: journal, specialized team, international meetings. Now let us have a look at the subjects treated. As the studies in question are centred on the past and do not relate to one subject of research only, they present a considerable diversity. All the aspects of demography are dealt with.

153. In France, an ambitious project launched about fifteen years ago is nearing completion. Its purpose was to reconstitute the population trend in France from the beginning of the eighteenth century, by means of a perusal of parish registers. A sample of parishes was chosen by lot, and data on the life and death of the families which had made up the population of those parishes was patiently assembled. Only some of the results have so far been published. The moment is approaching when a mass of unpublished results will become available, which will throw new light on the trend of mortality and fertility rates at a time when the practice of birth control had only just begun. In the course of this reconstitution of the past, special methods of analysis were gradually developed and a textbook for researchers wishing to undertake similar studies has been published. Besides the above-mentioned over-all study of France, a number of regional research projects have been undertaken by individual researchers.

154. Similar studies are taking place in the United Kingdom. A specialized research group has been formed at Cambridge (Cambridge Group for the History of Population and Social Structure). An important demographic study of the peers of the Realm in the United Kingdom was published recently by the Population Investigation Committee of the London School of Economics. In addition, a work published in Great Britain by D. V. Glass and D. E. C. Eversley,[38] gives an excellent selection of the studies conducted in most parts of the world.

155. The Office of Population Research of Princeton University has undertaken a study, by small administrative districts, of the population trend in the various European countries during the nineteenth century. The object of the study is to show where and how the decline in the fertility rate in this part of the world began.

Mention should also be made of the studies being carried out at the University of California (Berkeley), while at the University of Pennsylvania (Philadelphia) work is in progress on a history of world population.

156. The specialized research team recently formed in France has just begun its work. The research programme covers the following six points:

It is proposed to extend to 1866 the nominal record of the population of 40 villages already studied for the period 1670 to 1829 in the research mentioned above. A study of the causes of death at the end of the eighteenth and beginning of the nineteenth centuries will be undertaken with the aid of various medical and statistical documents. A reconstitution is to be effected of families formed in the eighteenth century in Rouen and about a hundred neighbouring parishes. An examination of Catholic registers of the sixteenth and early seventeenth centuries is expected to provide methodological information for a more general study of the same kind. The geographical distribution of the French population from 1600 to the present time will be determined through the use, in particular, of tax rolls. This piece of research will lead to the publication of departmental dictionaries in which the administrative history of each department (administrative sub-division of France) will be found. Lastly, an anthropological study of the French male population in the nineteenth century is to be undertaken, based on documents concerning recruitment for military service. All the foregoing studies are already under way.

157. In connexion with these researches, France is continuing the publication of forgotten works of the past relating to demography. In 1967, an annotated edition of the works of Boisguilbert was published. This important French official belonging to the reign of Louis XIV expressed during his life-time some very shrewd ideas about the links between economic and social development and population trends which, considering the time when they were put forward, seem astonishingly up to date.

A French edition of the works of the German demographer Süssmilch, who published in 1741 his masterpiece *Die Göttliche Ordnung*, is in preparation. It should be noted that Süssmilch's works are not to be found anywhere except in the big national libraries.

158. Similarly, the International Union for the Scientific Study of Population is preparing for publication a work by the Dutch demographer Kerseboom – a pioneer in the establishment of mortality tables.

159. We may also mention the forthcoming publication in France of a study of demographic ideas in the nineteenth century, as seen through French literature.

Use of defective data

We now come to a series of studies of an entirely different kind.

160. The importance of demographic factors in the economic and social advancement of the developing countries has led demographers in those countries and demographers working in the international organizations to consider the use made of the mass of demographic statistics collected over the years in those parts of the world. For a long time it was thought that these data were of too poor a quality to yield any significant information on the demographic situation in those regions.

161. The advances made in demographic analysis have led to a revision of this attitude and, gradually, a new system of methods has been devised enabling the best possible use to be made of defective data. In this respect, the Population Division of the United Nations has acted as a powerful catalysing agent for the researches undertaken. Two books have lately been published summing up the results so far achieved. The development of these researches was due to circumstances and it is unlikely that they will be extended much in the future. The efforts made to improve the quality of demographic statistics are beginning to bear fruit and there are grounds for hoping that sound data will soon be available.

162. One of the fundamental aims of this work on the analysis of defective data was to establish 'sample situations' and to compare with these situations the countries under investigation. In this way, some series of sample mortality-rate tables have been drawn up representing the different stages through which mankind passed when its mortality-rate fell. Here, the Population Division of the United Nations blazed the trail by publishing a series of such tables in a single dimension. Further series in several dimensions followed (France, usa). Similar researches have been undertaken in the matter of fertility, but they are less advanced.

163. Theoretical considerations have also played their part. The concept of stable population evolved before the last war by Alfred J. Lotka has been debated afresh and two new concepts have emerged – those of 'quasi-stable' and 'nearly stable' populations. The former are empirical populations, that is, populations arrived at by maintaining the fertility rate constant and varying the mortality rate over the area defined by the sample tables just referred to. It has been observed that these populations differ little from the stable populations.

164. Nearly stable populations are populations that are invariable in their composition by age. It has been shown that, at any given moment, the relations existing between the various characteristics of these populations are the same as those existing in the case of stable populations.

165. The populations of the developing countries fulfil approximately one or other of the conditions which served for the elaboration of the two concepts of

population, 'quasi-stable' and 'nearly stable'. It will readily be realized how these concepts can be used for the analysis of the demographic data assembled in those countries.

Electronic computers
166. We must also mention another type of research, the originality of which resides in the use of new media of investigation – electronic computers.

As in the case of research in historical demography, this type relates to all the sectors of demography and the only reason for placing it in a special category is the novelty of the methods employed.

167. Electronic computers have made possible what are now known as 'simulations'. The word is a new one, but the idea is extremely old, and the demographers who formerly worked out projections using the classical methods of calculation were really doing nothing other than simulation. They observed what would happen to a population subjected to a given set of demographic conditions. Because of the inadequate means of calculation then available, the data had perforce to be simplified. The use of electronic computers now permits of all possible complications.

The advances made in demographic analysis and the establishment of 'sample situations' have therefore made it possible to construct 'models' bearing an even stronger resemblance to actual situations.

168. But that is not all. Thanks to computers, we have been able to pass from determinist models to probabilist models. What is happening in a population where decisions are taken at the individual level is actually simulated. It is sufficient to introduce laws of probability into the computer; the machine then produces haphazardly the demographic events corresponding to those probabilities. This enables us to observe not only the trend of average values (which the determinist models already made possible) but also their variation.

169. By modifying the laws of probability, different simulations are obtained and in this way the demographer brings into being the conditions of a pseudo-experiment. In real life, the behaviour of individuals is modified by population trends and, as little is known about these modifications, simulation by electronic computer cannot be regarded as a true experiment. However, here again progress is possible and, indeed, probable.

170. It is also thanks to electronic computers that research based on a 'comparison of documents' has recently been able to emerge from the handicraft state in which it was hitherto confined through lack of facilities. The principle of this research resides in the comparison of documents drawn up on different occasions. We have already mentioned in connexion with mortality rates a research project in France and another in the USA where this method is being used. In the case of both projects, death certificates are compared with census returns. Some Canadian demographers have set out to compare in the same way successive

censuses from the beginning of the French occupation of the territory. The computer provides a document in which each inhabitant appears as many times as he or she was included in a census, and in the case of each census the characteristics recorded are available. Consequently, by following a given individual throughout the course of his or her life, any particular census can be corrected by another.

Comparison in time is not the only kind possible. One can also compare at a single given date documents drawn up by various administrations.

Population genetics

171. We now propose to touch on present research in population genetics.

In the early stages of population genetics three names stand out: R. A. Eisher, J. B. S. Haldane and S. Wright. In the direction indicated by them, important research was carried out by mathematicians who gradually became more interested in refining equations than in studying their biological significance. Present-day research relies on ever more elaborate mathematical techniques but becomes less and less applicable to actual cases. The danger is all the greater in that the concepts used are often ambiguous: the fact that such highly technical problems as the 'genetic load' or the calculation of 'lethal equivalents' have given rise to passionate controversy shows how important it is that an attempt should be made to clarify ideas and terms.

Over the last twenty years, a new approach has been provided by G. Malécot. His replacement of questions of population genetics in their proper mathematical context, that of probability, has given rise to research concerned more particularly at the present time with a clarification of concepts.

Simultaneously with this theoretical research, practical work 'on the spot' is in progress with the object of measuring the genic or genotypical structures of actual populations; this work is particularly directed to the 'experimental populations' constituted by isolates, that is, more or less isolated human groups, in respect of which there is some hope of being able to furnish figures in support of theoretical parameters – selection coefficients, consanguinity coefficients, panmixian deviation, etc.

But the findings of such research are often unreliable. Since these measurements relate to populations, it is becoming increasingly clear that use should be made in them of demographic techniques; current research is concerned with clearly defining the kind of contribution that population genetics may expect to receive from demography.

X. A FEW CLOSING REMARKS

172. From the foregoing it will undoubtedly have been noted that the objectives pursued by demographic research have a bearing on the daily life of individuals. This is not always the case with the other human sciences, whose lines of research seem sometimes to be far removed from everyday life.

173. This practical aspect of demographic research is not entirely to its advantage. Observing that the demographers' areas of research are so closely akin to his own preoccupations, the man-in-the-street may be tempted to think that there is no need to be a specialist to discuss these problems. Whereas no one would dream of casting doubt on the assertions of an astrophysicist explaining the result of his observations on the sun, for example, it is not unusual to see the conclusions of demographic research called in question by persons who have no authority in the matter. Since these conclusions are generally based on 'probabilities', it is, by definition, always possible to quote particular cases which contradict them. The would-be demographer is bound to be led into such misconceptions.

174. One way of remedying this unfortunate situation would be to give demographic training a place of its own in education. So far, this training has never been very well integrated in the various educational systems, and it is understandable that public opinion should not take with all due seriousness the results of research which even the universities long regarded as unworthy of being taught as a separate subject in its own right. Considerable progress has been made in this direction over the past few years, but much still remains to be done.

175. Since the subjects of demographic research are closely related to actual situations, their variety necessitates, as a rule, a choice influenced by the conditions of the moment. Moreover, it is often at this price that it is possible to obtain the necessary funds for research. For instance, a team of demographers working in Asia will not direct its research along the same lines as another team working in Europe. The first team will tend to concern itself with problems raised by the very high fertility rate of the countries in which it is living, while the second will rather study those raised by the decline in the fertility rate, such, for example, as the ageing of populations.

This diversity of interests might lead to a belief in the existence, among demographers, of different schools of thought throughout the world. In fact, this diversity does no more than indicate differences in demographic situations and, contrary to what may be observed in other human sciences, demographers all agree on the content of their science.

NOTES

1. We are referring here to sexual reproduction, with the marriage institution as a natural consequence.
2. We have here an essential difference between human sciences and those concerned with inanimate matter. With the latter, you cannot descend below a certain 'quantum' of action. Of course, it is not impossible that one day we shall discover that human science phenomena are, in their turn, 'quantified'.
3. Conversely, it can be asked if population censuses have not been used sometimes to change the way of thinking of the population concerned, for instance, in the case of a new nation. The fact of being counted creates a bond between the inhabi-

tants, strengthens the feeling of belonging to a group. Possibly it is this idea which is expressed in Article II of the United States' Constitution.

4. In the survey, the 58 % is found with a margin for error which depends on the size of the sample. We know, for instance, that it is situated between 55 and 61 %. By questioning the entire population, we know the exact percentage. It will be 58.2 %, for example. We will have gained in precision; will have a better idea of the population's 'situation'. But opinion will have been affected to such an extent that we shall no longer know where we are at the end of the total survey. We should no longer know anything about the population 'rate' in relation to the phenomenon being examined.

5. Of course, the converse is also true.

6. In small populations, even without the differential choice of the marriage partner or the differential fertility, mortality or migration rates, the mere operation of chance causes a variation in the proportion of genes – what is known as genetic deviation. However, the effect of this is only noticeable in *very* small populations.

7. We assume that first cousins and descendants of first cousins are included in the inter-marriage area.

8. Furthermore, we know little about the short-term infertility which affects a girl immediately after puberty.

9. More exactly 750,000 oöcytes, forerunners of the ovules.

10. At the socio-biological stage, short-term variations are observable in the birth-rate, even if only, for example, seasonal variations. They are then due, seemingly, to modifications in the intra-uterine mortality rate, whether provoked or unprovoked. In the former case, to which may be added infanticide, we have already a partial psycho-sociological determinant of fertility.

11. It might well be asked in this connexion, if it is not such tensions which have lent so much prominence to discussions concerning abortion during the last few years.

12. It is known, moreover, that sexual intercourse prior to marriage is by no means a rarity, and a strong proportion of first-borns are the result of pre-marriage conceptions. What is less well known is to what extent such pre-marital relations are the result or the cause of marriage.

13. The outside environment can also be changed. For instance, malaria has been banished from vast tracts of country by the use of powerful insecticides. On the other hand, economic development can also have evil consequences: thus irrigation has encouraged the spread of diseases such as bilharziasis.

14. It can be conceded that the ancestor who no longer produces anything directly still participates in production by being, for example, 'the one who knows the group's past', provided that this past is regarded by the group as useful to its daily life.

15. The type of hospital depends, for example, on the mortality rate. Diseases that call for attention differ according to whether the mortality rate is high or low.

16. Unless gifts are received from a foreign country.

17. We are referring here to the income of a private citizen. The global capital income is very much higher, but only a fraction of this is distributed to the owner of the capital. This fraction normally represents 4 or 5 % on the capital.

18. By resorting to the world capital market it is possible to exceed this percentage. But, obviously, not all countries can do this.

19. A part of a State's or collectivity's financial resources can also be derived from capital income.

20. Certain countries have exceeded this percentage.

21. Seen from the angle of the developing countries, 1 % of the national revenue of the wealthy countries represents 10 % of the revenue of the poor countries – which is far from being a negligible amount.

22. We mean here a practical possibility, for before electronic computers existed it was of course already possible to compare two census returns one by one. But this was a lengthy process and only very rarely undertaken. Now, with the aid of

electronic computers, such comparison can be extended to entire populations.
23. The aeroplane also plays its part, but it seems unlikely to become a means of mass transport.
24. Changes could of course be made in the manner of carrying out censuses, so that they could also be used for observation purposes. But it is now clear that they will never be able to take the place of sample investigations.
25. Historical demography has made great strides within the last few years. We shall return to this subject when dealing with research now in progress.
26. This institute ceased its activities, however, some years ago.
27. This is what Elizabeth Pfeil wrote in 1958 in a booklet published by Unesco: 'At the present moment, no interest is taken in demography in Germany... Yet between 1920 and 1930 very active research in this science had produced important results. But, later on, national socialism made demography serve its own political party ends, which interfered with progress'.
28. Of course this attempted standardization must not be carried too far. It was very quickly realized that a complete standardization of ideas and definitions would be illusory and, indeed, misleading, having regard to the varied economic, social, cultural and political conditions in the various countries.
29. We only mention here the Specialized Agencies with a direct interest in population questions.
30. This Committee was created in August, 1963 by the Economic and Social Council following a report of the United Nations Conference on the Application of Science and Technology for the Benefit of the Less Developed Areas (Geneva, February, 1963). It comprises 15 members.
31. In 1967, a European Working Group on Social Demography was set up by the United Nations Office in Geneva, whose task is to bring about such co-ordination.
32. Speech delivered by Marcolino G. Candau, M.D., Director-General of WHO at the forty-second conference of the Milbank Memorial Fund in New York, October, 1967.
33. Speech delivered by Alexander Robertson at the forty-second conference of the Milbank Memorial Fund in New York, October, 1967.
34. Dates indicate year of publication.
35. *Asian Drama: An Inquiry into the Poverty of Nations*, London, 1969.
36. The Higher Education Research Group.
37. These figures are given merely as an example. They would obviously vary from one country to another, though it is probable that the ratio mentioned here would remain the same.
38. *Population in History*, London, 1965. *Essays in Historical Demography*.

REFERENCES *(numbers refer to paragraphs in text)*

2. MOHEAU, *Recherches et considérations sur la population de la France. 1778*, Paris, 1912.
4. P. VINCENT, 'La mortalité des vieillards', *Population* (2), 1951, p. 181 ff.
14. J. SUTTER, *L'eugénique*, Paris, P.U.F., 1966. (Coll. 'Travaux et Documents' de l'I.N.E.D., Cahier no. 11.)
   G. MALECOT, *Probabilités et hérédité*, Paris, P.U.F., 1966. (Coll. 'Travaux et Documents' de l'I.N.E.D., Cahier no. 47.)
   CHING CHUN LI, *Population Genetics*, Chicago, 1955.
   C. STERN, *Principles of Human Genetics*, San Francisco-London, 1960.
   O. KEMPTHORNE, *An Introduction to Genetic Statistics*, New York-London-Sydney, 1957.
15. J. BOURGEOIS-PICHAT, *Relations entre la mortalité foeto-infantile et la fécondité*. Contribution to the United Nations World Population Conference, held at Belgrade, 30 August to 10 September 1965.
   F. E. FRENCH and J. M. BIERMAN, *Probabilities of Foetal Mortality*, Washington, Public Health Reports, 1962.

66   *Jean Bourgeois-Pichat*

S. SHAPIRO, E. W. JONES and P. M. DENSEN, 'A Life Table of Pregnancy Termination and Correlates of Foetal Loss', *Milbank Memorial Fund Quarterly* 40 (1), Jan. 1962.

C. TIETZE and C. MARTIN, 'Foetal Deaths, Spontaneous and Induced, in the Urban White Population of the United States', *Population Studies* 11 (2), Nov. 1957, pp. 170–176. Tables.

W. TAYLOR, 'On the Methodology of Measuring the Probability of Foetal Death in a Prospective Study', *Human Biology* 36 (2), May 1964, pp. 86–103. Tables, graphs.

H. NEWCOMBE, 'Risk of Foetal Deaths to Mothers of Different ABO and RH Blood Types', *The American Journal of Human Genetics* 15 (4), Dec. 1963, pp. 449–464. Tables, graphs, bibliogr.

L. HENRY, 'Mortalité intra-utérine et fécondabilité', *Population* (5), 1964, pp. 899–940. Tables, graphs, appendices.

E. HAMMOND, 'Studies in Foetal and Infant Mortality. I. A Methodological Approach to the Definition of Perinatal Mortality. II. Differentials in Mortality by Sex and Race', *American Journal of Public Health* 45 (7), July 1965, pp. 1012–1023; 55 (8), Aug. 1965, pp. 1152–1163.

J. H. DE HAAS-POSTHUMA, *Prenatale Sterfte in Nederland. Onderzoek naar factoren, die de prenatale sterfte beïnvloeden*, Assen, Van Gorcum, 1962, 223 + 93 p. Tables in appendix, bibliogr.

R. FREEDMAN, L. COOMBS and J. FREEDMAN, 'Social Correlates of Foetal Mortality', *The Milbank Memorial Fund Quarterly* 44 (3), July 1966, 1st Part, pp. 327–344. Bibliogr.

L. BAUMGARTNER, H. WALLACE, E. LANDSBERG and V. PESSIN, 'The Inadequacy of Routine Reporting of Foetal Deaths', *American Journal of Public Health* 39 (12), Dec. 1949, pp. 1549–1552.

M. C. SHEPS and J. C. RIDLEY (eds.), *Public Health and Population Changes. Current Research Issues*, Pittsburgh, 1965, 557 p. Tables, graphs.

17. J. BOURGEOIS-PICHAT, 'Les facteurs de la fécondité non dirigée', *Population* (3), May-June 1965, pp. 383–424.

P. VINCENT, 'Réflexions sur une cause possible en stérilité conjugale: l'incompatibilité sanguine par rapport au facteur Rh.', *Journal de la Société de Statistique de Paris*, Jan.-Febr. 1948, pp. 6–28. Bibliogr.

ASHLEY, *Adolescent Sterility. A Study in the Comparative Physiology of the Infecundity of the Adolescent Organism in Mammals and Man*, Springfield, 1946, 148 p. Bibliogr.

D. GALLEGO and G. DE ALLEZ, 'Esterilidad voluntaria e involuntaria de la mujer española', *Revista internacional de sociología* 12 (47), July-Sept. 1954, pp. 537–559.

FREEDMAN, WHELPTON and CAMPBELL, *Family Planning, Sterility and Population Growth*, New York-Toronto-London, McGraw-Hill, 1959, 515 p.

BREZNIK, 'Sterility of First Marriages', in: *Studies in Fertility and Social Mobility. Proceedings of the International Demographic Symposium held November 20–30, 1962 at the Hungarian Academy of Sciences*, Budapest, 1964, pp. 19–26.

W. GRABILL and P. GLICK, 'Demographic and Social Aspects of Childlessness: Census Data', *The Milbank Memorial Fund Quarterly* 37 (1), Jan. 1959, pp. 60–86.

GRIFFITH, 'Gonorrhea and Fertility in Uganda', *The Eugenics Review* 55 (2), July 1963, pp. 103–108. Tables, fig., bibliogr.

18. A. RETEL-LAURENTIN, 'Influence de certaines maladies sur la fécondité. Un exemple africain', *Population* (5), 1967, pp. 841–860.

M. SAVORGNAN, 'I matrimoni, senza prole e le sterilità', *Rivista italiana di economia, demografia e statistica* 15 (3/4), July-Dec. 1961, pp. 261–268.

MEUWISSEN, 'Human Infertility in Ghana', *Fertility and Sterility* 18 (2), Mar.-Apr. 1967, pp. 223–231. Bibliogr.

R. COOK, 'Lethal Genes. A Factor in Fertility', *Eugenical News* 38 (3), Sept. 1953, pp. 49–55. Bibliogr.

P. B. MEDAWAR and D. V. GLASS (eds.), *A Discussion on Demography*, Cambridge, University Printing House, 1963, 255 p. (Reprint from the *Proceedings of the Royal Society Bulletin* 159, 1963.)

19. L. Henry, 'Mesure du temps mort en fécondité naturelle', *Population* (3), 1964, pp. 485–514.

    K. Srinivasan, 'A Probability Model Applicable to the Study of Inter-Live Birth-Intervals and Random Segment of the Same', *Population Studies* 21 (1), July 1967, pp. 63–70.

    R. Potter, 'Birth Intervals: Structure and Change', *Population Studies* 17 (2), Nov. 1963, pp. 155–166. Tables, bibliogr.

    J. C. Ridley, M. Sheps, J. Lingner and J. Menken, 'The Effects of Changing Mortality on Natality. Some Estimations from a Simulation Model', *The Milbank Memorial Fund Quarterly* 45 (1), Jan. 1967, pp. 77–97. Tables, graphs, bibliogr.

    H. Leridon, 'Les intervalles entre naissances', *Population* (5), 1967, Sept.-Oct. 1967, pp. 821–840. Tables, graphs.

    H. Hyrenius, 'Fertility and Reproduction in a Swedish Population Group without Family Limitation', *Population Studies* 12 (2), Nov. 1958, pp. 121–130.

    G. E. Huntington and J. A. Hostetler, 'A Note on Nursing Practices in an American Isolate with a High Birth Rate', *Population Studies* 19 (3), Mar. 1966, pp. 319–324.

    N. Federici, 'Caratteristiche demografiche di alcuni gruppi di Caramai e di un gruppo di Ebrei dell'Europa Orientale', *Genus* 9 (1/4), 1950–1952, pp. 138–175.

    K. Dandekar, 'Intervals Between Confinements', *Eugenics Quarterly* 6 (3), Sept. 1959, pp. 180–186.

    S. P. Jain, *Post-partum Amenorrhea in Indian Women.* Communication to the Congress of the i.u.s.s.p., Sydney (Australia), 21–25 Aug. 1967.

    R. G. Potter, J. E. Gordon, M. Parker and J. B. Myon, 'A Case Study of Birth Interval Dynamics', *Population Studies* 19 (1), July 1965, p. 89.

    C. Tietze, 'The Effect of Breast-Feeding on the Rate of Conception', pp. 129–136, in: *World Population Congress* (New York, 1961), Vol. ii., London, i.u.s.s.p., 1963, 579 p.

    B. S. Sehgal and R. S. Singh, *Breast-Feeding, Amenorrhea, and Rates of Conception in Women.* Mimeogr.

    S. Biswas, 'A Study of Amenorrhea after Childbirth and its Relationship to Lactation Period', *Indian Journal of Public Health* 7 (1) Jan. 1963, p. 9.

    S. Matsumoto, *Menstrual Cycle and its Abnormality.* Mimeogr. 1962. [Japanese.]

    S. Matsumoto, *Resumption of Menstruation after Childbirth.* Mimeogr. [Japanese.]

    B. M. Ghosh, 'Feeding Habits of Infants and Children in South India (in 600 Families)', *The Indian Journal of Medical Research* 54, Sept. 1966.

    K. Dandekar, *Demographic Survey on Six Rural Communities*, Poona (India), Gokhale Institute of Politics and Economics, 1959.

    M. C. Sheps, 'An Analysis of Reproductive Patterns in an American Isolate', *Population Studies* 19 (1), July 1965, p. 78.

    G. E. Huntington and J. A. Hostetler, 'A Note on Nursing Practices in an American Isolate with a High Birth Rate', *Population Studies* 19 (3) Mar. 1966, p. 321.

21. R. G. Potter, Jr., 'Length of the Fertile Period', *The Milbank Memorial Fund Quarterly* 39 (1), Jan. 1961.

    A. Kusukawa, 'A Demographic Model of Fertility Related to Coïtus for Populations Not Practising Family Limitation', *Kyushu Journal of Medical Science* 4 (6), Dec. 1963.

    Kinsey, *Sexual Behavior in the Human Female*, Philadelphia-London, Institute for Sex Research, Indiana University, 1953.

    N. Shinozaki, *Report on Sexual Life of Japanese*, Tokyo, The Institute of Population Problems, Welfare Ministry, July 1957.

    M. Nag, 'Factors Affecting Human Fertility in Non-Industrial Societies. A Cross-Cultural Study', *Yale University Publications in Anthropology 66*, 1962, pp. 3–227.

24. United Nations, Population Commission, *Activities of the Specialized Agencies in the Field of Population and Closely Related Affairs*, Document e/cn. 9/219/ Add. 1, 14th Session of the Population Commission, Geneva, 30 Oct. – 10 Nov. 1967.

25. J. Bourgeois-Pichat, *Allocution d'ouverture à la Conférence démographique européenne de Strasbourg*, 30 août-6 sept. *1966*, Document c.d.e. (66) 5/2.

29. *Trends in the Study of Morbidity and Mortality*, Geneva, World Health Organization, 1965. 196 p. Illustr. (Public Health Papers, no. 27.)

    J. Sutter and J. M. Goux, 'Les équivalents létaux et la mesure démographique de la mortalité', *Population* (5), Sept.-Oct. 1965, pp. 829–850.

    N. Federici, 'Evolution de la mortalité: ses causes et ses conséquences. Rétrospective et situation actuelle', in: *Conférence démographique européenne*, Strasbourg, 30 août – 6 sept. 1966, 6 p. (Documents officiels de la Conférence, s.l.n.d. Vol. 3., c.d.e. (66) D 3).

    E. Garanti, 'Evolution de la mortalité, ses causes et ses conséquences. Perspectives'. in: *Conférence démographique européenne*, Strasbourg, 30 août-6 sept. 1966, 6 p. (Documents officiels de la Conférence, s.l.n.d. Vol. 3. c.d.e. (66), D 4).

30. J. Bourgeois-Pichat, 'Essai sur la mortalité 'biologique' de l'homme', *Population* (3), July-Sept. 1952, pp. 381–394.

32. E. Desanti, *Médecine sociale, médecine préventive et logistique médicale*, Paris, 1967, 403 p. Tables, bibliogr.

    B. MacMahon, T. F. Pucg and H. Ipsen, *Epidemiologic Methods*, Boston-Toronto, Little Brown, 1960, 302 p. Tables, fig., graphs.

33. T. McKeown, 'Medicine and World Population', pp. 25–40, in: *Public Health and Population Change. Current Research Issues*. Pittsburgh, 1965, 557 p. Tables, graphs.

36. M. Hauge, B. Harvald and B. Degnbol, 'Hereditary Factors in Longevity', pp. 190–192, in: *Age With a Future*. Proceedings of the 6th International Congress of Gerontology. (Copenhagen, 1963).

38. B. Benjamin, 'Actuarial Methods of Mortality Analysis: Adaptation to Changes in the Age and Cause Pattern', pp. 38–65, in: *A Discussion on Demography* (arranged by P. B. Medawar and D. V. Glass, 15–18 Nov. 1962), Cambridge, 1963, 225 p.

    R. Pressat, 'Vieillesse et vieillissement. Le point de vue du démographe', *Le Concours médical* 1, 6 Jan. 1968, pp. 107–109. Tables.

39. S. Ledermann, *Alcool, alcoolisme, alcoolisation*, Vol. 11: *Mortalité, accidents du travail*, Paris, p.u.f., 1964, 613 p. Bibliogr. (Coll. 'Travaux et Documents' de l'i.n.e.d., Cahier no. 41.)

    Mortality from Diseases Associated with Smoking: United States, 1950–1964, Washington, Department of Health, Education and Welfare, 1966, 45 p. Tables, graphs.

42. A. Sauvy, *Théorie générale de la population*, Vol. 1: *Economie et croissance*, Paris, p.u.f., 1963; Vol. 11: *La vie des populations*, Paris, p.u.f., 1966.

    'L'évolution du coût des soins', *Notes et Documents de la F.N.O.S.S.* 14, 1964, 39 p. Tables. 'Investment in Human Beings', *Journal of Political Economy* 70 (5, Part 2), Oct. 1962, pp. 1–157.

43. J. Bourgeois-Pichat, 'Pour une éthique de l'an 2000', in: *La France contemporaine. Les doctrines, les idées et les faits*, Monaco, Union européenne d'éditions, 1967 [four illustrated volumes].

    G. L'Eltore, *Indications préliminaires pour une sociologie des phénomènes pathologiques humains (socio-pathologie)*, Rome, Quintily, [s.d.], 58 p. Tables, map. (xviith Congress of the International Institute of Sociology, Beirut, 23–29 Sept. 1957.)

47. M. Berstein and M. Martinez-Gustin, 'Physical and Psychological Variation and the Sex Ratio', *The Journal of Heredity* 52 (3), May-June 1961, pp. 109–112. Bibliogr.

    L. A. Goodman, 'Some Possible Effects of Birth Control on the Human Sex Ratio', *Annals of Human Genetics* 25 (1), *May* 1961, pp. 75–81.

    A. S. Parkes, 'The Sex Ratio in Human Population', pp. 90–99, in: *Man and His Future* (A Ciba Foundation Volume), London, 1963, 410 p. Bibliogr.

    J. R. Seagrave, 'A Note on Sex-Predetermination and Population Growth', *Population Review* 11 (1), Jan. 1967, pp. 44–46. Bibliogr.

52. J. Magaud, 'Equivalent travail d'une production. Nouvelle méthode de calcul et de prévision', *Population* 11 (2), Mar.-Apr. 1967, pp. 193–238.

S. ENKE, 'Speculations on Population Growth and Economic Development', *The Quarterly Journal of Economics* 71 (1), Feb. 1957, pp. 19–35.

Economia e popolazione, Atti del Seminario di demografia tenuto nell'anno academico 1963–1964 a cura del Prof. Pierfrancesco Bandettini, Firenze, Scuola di statistica dell'Università, 1965, 115 p. Tables, bibliogr.

R. EASTERLIN, 'Effects of Population Growth on the Economic Development of Developing Countries', *The Annals of the American Academy of Political and Social Science* 369, Jan. 1967, pp. 98–108. Tables, bibliogr.

G. LOYO, *Población y desarrollo económico*, México-London (tipografía), 1963, 233 p.

G. MORTARA, *Economia della popolazione. Analizi dell relazioni tra fenomeni economici e fenomeni demografici*, Torino, Unione tipografico editrice torinese, 1960, 514 p. (Trattato italiano di economia, Vol. III, U.T.E.T.)

A. SAUVY, 'Investissements démographiques et investissements économiques', pp. 136–141, in: *International Population Conference* (Vienna, 1959), Vienna, 1959, 735 p.

VARGA, 'Tervgazdasag es demográfia' [Economic planning and demography], *Demográfia* 5 (3) 1962, pp. 315–324.

54. J. BONIFACE, C. QUIN and A. GAUSSEL, *Les consommateurs*, Paris, 1965, 192 p. Tables, graphs, bibliogr.

55. J. BENARD, *Vues sur l'économie et la population de la France jusqu'en 1970*, Paris, P.U.F., 1953, 307 p. (Coll. 'Travaux et Documents' de l'I.N.E.D., Cahier no. 17.)

'L'évolution du nombre des ménages entre 1954 et 1962 et ses perspectives', *Etudes et Conjoncture* (4), Apr. 1966, pp. 3–102.

Perspectives d'évolution de la population de la France, population totale, population active et scolaire, ménages', *Etudes statistiques* (3), June-Sept. 1964, pp. 155–220. Tables.

56. *L'évolution démographique de 1965 à 1980 en Europe occidentale et en Amérique du Nord / Demographic Trends 1965–1980 in Western Europe and North America*, Paris, O.C.D.E./O.E.C.D., 1966, 116 p. Supplement: *Rapport par pays / Report by Country*, Paris, O.C.D.E./O.E.C.D., 1966, 355 p.

N. NOVACCO, 'Prévision pour l'année 1975 sur la population italienne selon la qualification professionnelle et le degré d'instruction', pp. 493–508, in: *World Population Conference* (New York, 1961), Vol. II, London, I.U.S.S.P., 1963, 597 p.

Problems of Human Resources Planning in Latin America and in the Mediterranean Regional Project Countries. Long-Term Forecasts of Manpower Requirements and Educational Policies. Report of the Seminar held in Lima in March 1965, and complementary documents. Paris, O.E.C.D., 1967, 279 p. Diagrams, tables.

58. J. MAGAUD, 'Perspectives régionales des ménages', *Population* 11 (1), Jan.-Feb. 1967, pp. 117–121.

'Perspectives régionales de la population active', *Études et Conjoncture* (1), Jan. 1966, pp. 77–131. Tables.

'Perspectives démographiques régionales en 1970 et 1978', *Études et Conjoncture* (4), Apr. 1965, pp. 85–165. Tables, maps.

M. LIVI BACCI, *La dinamica demografica delle regioni italiane. Previsioni al 1981*, Rome, 1964, 280 p.

75. Y. TUGAULT, 'Migrations internes en France de 1954 à 1962 selon l'importance des localités', *Population* 12 (3), May-June 1967, pp. 455–482.

Report of the Ad Hoc Committee of Experts on Programmes in Demographic Aspects of Urbanization, Sydney (Australia), 29 Aug.-2 Sept. 1967. United Nations, Doc. E/CN 9/218.

Le migrazioni interne in Italia, Atti del Seminario di demografia tenuto nell'anno academico 1965–66 a cura del Prof. Massimo Livi Bacci, Firenze, Scuola di statistica dell'Università, 1967, 297 p. Tables, graphs.

G. POURCHER, 'Un essai d'analyse par cohorte de la mobilité géographique et professionnelle', *Population* 11 (2), Mar.-Avril 1966, pp. 356–378.

D. FRIEDLANDER and R. J. ROSHIER, 'A Study of Internal Migration in England and

70   *Jean Bourgeois-Pichat*

Wales, Part 1: Geographical Patterns of Internal Migration 1851–1951,' *Population Studies* 19 (3), Mar. 1966, pp. 239–279.

D. FRIEDLANDER and R. J. ROSHIER, 'A Study of Internal Migration in England and Wales, Part II: Recent Internal Migrants – Their Movements and Characteristics', *Population Studies* 20 (1), July 1966, pp. 45–59.

H. SHRYOCK, *Population Mobility within the U.S.*, Chicago, Community and Family Study Center, 1964, 470 p. Tables, graphs.

H. T. ELDRIDGE, *Net Intercensal Migration of States and Geographic Divisions of the U.S. 1950–1960: Methodological and Substantive Aspects*, Philadelphia, 1965, 225 p. Tables, maps.

75.–80. M. LIVI BACCI, *La dinamica demografica delle regioni italiane. Previsioni al 1981*, Rome, 1964, 280 p., Tables, graphs.

A. PREDETTI, *Le componenti economische sociali e demografiche della mobilità interna della popolazione italiana*, Milan, 1965, 143 p. Tables, bibliogr.

J. BEAUJEU-GARNIER AND G. CHABOT, *Traité de géographie urbaine*, Paris, 1963, 493 p. Bibliogr.

V. BRUNO, *Lineamenti demo-economici dei communi italiani per gradi di urbanità e di ruralità*, Milan, 1965, 207 p. Tables, graphs, bibliogr.

77. R. TRUGGVESON, *Urbanisering och tätortsutveckling 1951–1960. Demografiska undersökningar*, Lund, 1967, 328 p. Tables, graphs.

P. HAUSER AND L. SCHNORE (eds.), *The Study of Urbanization*, New York-London-Sydney, 1965, 554 p.

E. SONNINO, 'Le caratteristische socio-demografische degli immigrati ed il loro apporto allo sviluppo di una grande città: il caso di Roma', in: *Le migrazioni interne in Italia*, Atti del seminario tenuto nell'anno academico 1965–1966, Firenze, 1967, 297 p. Bibliogr.

G. POURCHER, *Le peuplement de Paris: Origine régionale. [Compositions sociales. Attitudes et motivations*, Paris, P.U.F., 1964, 311 p. Tables, graphs, bibliogr. (Coll. 'Travaux et Documents' de l'I.N.E.D., Cahier no. 43.)

Report of the Ad Hoc Committee of Experts on Programmes in Demographic Aspects of Urbanization, cf. paragraph 75.

84. J. STOETZEL, 'Sociologie et démographie', *Population* (1), Jan.-Mar. 1946, pp. 79–89.

K. W. BACK, 'Frontiers in Demography and Social Psychology', *Demography* (1), 1967, pp. 90–97.

K. KULCSAR, 'Demográfia es szocologia' (Demography and sociology), *Demográfia* (2), 1962, pp. 188–205.

K. DAVIS, *Human Society*, London, 1949.

R. K. MERTON (ed.), *Sociology Today. Problems and Prospects*, New York, 1959.

86. A. GIRARD, *Le choix du conjoint*, Paris, P.U.F., 1964. (Coll. 'Travaux et Documents' de l'I.N.E.D., Cahier no. 44.)

92. L. HENRY, 'Problèmes de la recherche démographique moderne', *Population* (6), Nov.-Dec. 1966, pp. 1093–1114.

94. J. BRACKETT, 'Report on the One-Day Seminar on Computer Applications to Demography held at the Bureau of the Census in July 1964', *Demography* (2), 1965, pp. 627–629.

P. VINCENT, 'Application des ensembles électroniques à la recherche démographique', *Journal de la Société de Statistique de Paris* (7–9), 1964, pp. 135–164.

M. C. SHEPS and J. RIDLEY, 'An Analytic Simulation Model of Human Reproduction with Demographic and Biological Components', *Population Studies* 19 (3), March 1966, pp. 297–310.

H. HYRENIUS and I. ADOLFSSON, *A Fertility Simulation Model*, Göteborg, Demographic Institute, University of Göteborg, 1964.

A. JACQUARD, 'La reproduction humaine en régime malthusien. Un modèle de simulation par la méthode de Monte-Carlo', *Population* 11 (5), Sept.-Oct. 1967, pp. 897–920.

102. L. HENRY and M. FLEURY, *Des registres paroissiaux à l'histoire de la population: manuel de dépouillement et d'exploitation de l'état civil ancien*, Paris, I.N.E.D., 1956. (Repub-

lished in 1965 under the title: *Nouveau manuel de dépouillement et d'exploitation de l'état civil ancien.*)

117. *Demográfia.* Quarterly journal.
119. UNITED NATIONS, Statistical Commission, *Report on the 13th Session.* Official papers of the ECOSOC, 39th Session, Supplement no. 13.
120. UNITED NATIONS, Population Commission, *Report on the 13th Session.* Official papers of the ECOSOC, 39th Session, Supplement no. 9.
121. UNITED NATIONS, Population Commission, *Activities of the Specialized Agencies in the Field of Population and Closely Related Affairs*, Document E/CN. 9/219/Add. 1 of the 14th session of the Population Commission, Geneva, 30 October – 10 November 1967.
    UNESCO, *Report of The Special Committee of Experts on the Definition of Unesco's Responsibilities in the Field of Population*, Paris, UNESCO, Document SHC/CS/89/4, 20 Sept. 1967.
    'Population Trust Fund', *UN Monthly Chronicle*, Sept. 1967.
122. *Evolution démographique de 1965 à 1980 en Europe occidentale et en Amérique du Nord/ Demographic Trends 1965–1980 in Western Europe and North America*, Paris, O.C.D.E./O.E.C.D., 1966, 116p.
    Liaison Bulletin. Published by the Development Centre of O.E.C.D. (Liaison between development research and training institutes.)
    International Migrations. Quarterly journal of the Intergovernmental Committee for European Migration, The Hague.
    E. GARLOT, 'Une initiative du Conseil de l'Europe: la Conférence démographique européenne (30 août–6 sept. 1966)', *Population* 11 (3), May-June 1966, pp. 451–464.
    J. BAUDOT, 'Vues générales sur la première Conférence démographique européenne (30 août–6 sept. 1966)', *Population* 11 (6), Nov.-Dec. 1966, pp. 1115–1122.
124. *Report of the Interregional Workshop on Programmes of Training in the Field of Population* (Elsinore, Denmark, 19–30, June 1967), New York, United Nations, 1967, E/CN. 9/CONF/4/1.
    L. HENRY, *Leçons d'analyse démographique*, Paris, Centre de documentation universitaire, 1960 and 1964.
    L. HENRY, *Perspectives démographiques*, Paris, I.N.E.D., 1964.
    R. PRESSAT, *L'analyse démographique: méthodes, résultats, applications*, Paris, P.U.F., 1961.
    R. PRESSAT, *Principes d'analyse*, Paris, I.N.E.D., 1966.
    R. PRESSAT, *Pratique de la démographie. 30 sujets d'analyse*, Paris, Dunod, 1967.
    Methods of Estimating Basic Demographic Measures from Incomplete Data, Manual IV, New York, United Nations, sales no. 67.XIII.2.
126. P. HAUSER and O. D. DUNCAN (eds.), *The Study of Population. An Inventory and Appraisal*, Chicago-London, The University of Chicago Press, 1959.
    L. TABAH and J. VIET, *Démographie. Tendances actuelles et organisation de la recherche, 1955–1965*, Paris-The Hague, 1966 (Maison des sciences de l'homme, Publications Série B: Guides et répertoires).
127. *Human Resources for Health. Forty-Second Conference of the Milbank Memorial Fund* (October 17 to 19, 1967), New York, Milbank, Memorial Fund, 1967.
128. *Human Resources for Health* (op. cit.).
    'Social Science and Health Planning: Culture, Disease and Health Services in Colombia,' *Milbank Memorial Fund Quarterly* (2), 1968.
129. Various publications of the National Centre for Health Statistics. U.S. Public Health Services. Washington (D.C.).
130. J. S. WEINER, *International Biological Programme. Guide to Human Adaptability*, London, I.C.S.U., Special Committee for the International Biological Programme, 1965.
131. Bibliography in: W. A. WILSON, 'On Mortality Trends by Occupation and Social Class', European Demographic Conference, Strasbourg 30 Aug. – 6 Sept. 1966. (Official documents of the Conference, Vol. I.)

132. E. M. KITAGAWA and P. M. HAUSER, 'Social and Economic Differentials in Mortality in the United States, 1960. A Report on Methods'. Contribution to the Congress of the International Scientific Union for the Scientific Study of Population held in Ottawa, Canada (21–26 Aug. 1963), Liège, 1964.
     M. FEBVAY and M. CROZE, 'Contribution à l'étude de la mortalité infantile', *Etudes statistiques* (3), July-Sept. 1954.
133. G. CALOT and M. FEBVAY, 'La mortalité différentielle suivant le milieu social', *Etudes et Conjoncture* (11), Nov. 1965, pp. 75–159.
134. C. BLAYO and J. MAGAUD, 'Statistiques démographiques et organisation de la recherche en Hongrie', *Population* (3), May-June 1967, pp. 511–526.
135. *Statistical Bulletin*, New York, Metropolitan Life Insurance Company.
136. *Social and Genetic Influences on Life and Death*, Eugenic Society Symposium, Vol. 3. Proceedings of the 3rd Symposium of the Eugenic Society; introduction by Lord PLATT and A. S. PARKES, Edinburgh-London.
137. Bibliography in: T. E. REED, 'The Evidence for Natural Selection Due to Blood Groups', in: *World Population Conference* (Belgrade, 1965) (Vol. 11), United Nations, Sales no. 66.XIII.6.
138. UNITED NATIONS, Document E/CN/9/219/Add. 1 of 16 October, 1967. Prepared for the 14th session of the Population Commission (30 October – 10 November 1967).
139. Books and articles cited with reference to § 15, 17, 18, 19 and 21.
140. Bibliography in: N. B. RYDER and C. F. WESTOFF, 'The Trend of Excepted Parity in the United States: 1955, 1960, 1965', *Population Index* 33 (2), Apr.-June 1967.
     C. MIRO, 'Some Misconceptions Disproved: A Program of Comparative Fertility Surveys in Latin America', pp. 615–632, in: B. BERELSON *et al.*, *Family Planning and Population Programs. A Review of World Developments*, Chicago, 1966, 848 p.
     C. MIRO and F. RATH, 'Preliminary Findings of Comparative Fertility Surveys in Three Latin American Cities', *Milbank Memorial Fund Quarterly* 43, Oct. 1965, pp. 36–38.
     L. TABAH and R. SAMUEL, 'Preliminary Findings of a Survey on Fertility and Attitudes Toward Family Formation in Santiago (Chile)', in: C. V. KISER (ed.), *Milbank Memorial Fund Research in Family Planning*, Princeton, N. J., 1962, p. 289.
     Review *Estadística Panamena*, 1964.
     Selected Questionnaires on Knowledge, Attitudes and Practice of Family Planning, New York, 1967.
141. Publications of the National Committee on Maternal Health Inc., New York, with special emphasis on nos. 6 and 23 which contain an important bibliography.
     B. BERELSON and G. STEINER, *Human Behavior. An Inventory of Scientific Findings*, New York-Chicago, 1964.
     C. V. KISER (ed.), *Research in Family Planning*, Princeton (N. J.), 1962.
     Proceedings of the XVIIth International Conference on the Family (1–17 December 1966), New Delhi, Family Planning Association of India.
142. G. MYRDAL, *Asian Drama: An Inquiry into the Poverty of Nations*, London, 1969.
     UNITED NATIONS, *Causes and Consequences of the Demographic Evolution*, Sales no. 53. XIII.3.
     Le Tiers-Monde, Paris, P.U.F., 1961. (Coll. 'Travaux et Documents' de l'I.N.E.D., Cahier no. 39.)
143. J. MAGAUD, 'Equivalent travail d'une production. Nouvelle méthode de calcul et de prévision', *Population* (2), Mar.-Apr. 1967, pp. 193 and 238.
144. *America's Industrial and Occupational Manpower Requirements, 1964–1965*, Washington, United States Department of Labor, Bureau of Labor Statistics, Jan. 1966.
     M. HOROWITZ, M. ZYMELMAN and I. HERRNSTADT, *Manpower Requirements for Planning. An International Comparison Approach*, Boston (Mass.), Dec. 1966.
     C. VIMONT, P. d'HUGUES and M. PESLIER, 'La prévision de l'emploi dans le cadre du Vème Plan en France. La répartition de la population active par profession en 1970. Hypothèses de travail pour 1978', *Population* (3), May-June 1966, pp. 483 and 521.
     C. VIMONT, 'Les prévisions des besoins en main-d'œuvre dans les pays en voie de

développement. Aspects méthodologiques', pp. 173–181, in: *Contributed Papers*, Congress of the International Union for the Scientific Study of Population, 21–25 August, 1967, Sydney, Australia.

Higher Education: Government Statement on the Report of the Committee under the Chairmanship of Lord Robbins, London, H.M.S.O., 1963, 11 vols. + annexes.

Technology and the American Economy, Report of the National Commission on Technology, Automation and Economic Progress, Washington (D.C.), Government Printing Office, 1966.

Education, Human Resources and Development in Argentina, Paris, O.C.D.E., 1967.

Publications of the Institut für empirische Soziologie, Nurnberg, 7 Furdelgass, Bundesrepublik Deutschland.

M. R. POIGNANT (ed.), *Educational Planning in the U.S.S.R.*, Paris, Unesco, International Institute for Educational Planning, 1968.

C. VIMONT and G. RERAT, 'L'incidence du progrès technique sur la qualification ouvrière: une nouvelle méthode d'analyse', *Population* (3), 1966, pp. 541 ff.

C. VIMONT and G. RERAT, 'L'incidence du progrès technique sur la qualification professionnelle', *Population* (1), 1967, pp. 81 ff.

Demografía y Economía. Journal published by El Colegio de México, Guanajuato 125, México 7, D.F.

6–148. UNITED NATIONS, Population Commission, *Report on the 14th Session* (*30 Oct.–10 Nov. 1967*), United Nations, Document E/44.54 or E/CN.9/220.

149. *Annales de démographie historique*: 1964, 1965, 1966, 1967. Published by the Société de démographie historique.

153. Y. BLAYO and L. HENRY, 'Données démographiques sur la Bretagne et l'Anjou de 1740 à 1829', *Annales de démographie historique*, 1967.

L. HENRY, *Manuel de démographie historique*, Geneva, Paris, Proz, 1967.

154. D. E. C. EVERSLEY, P. LASLETT and E. A. WRIGLEY, *An Introduction to English Historical Demography*, London, 1966.

P. LASLETT, *An Age of Satire, 1660–1730. The Extent of Bastardy in Restoration England. An Essay of Literacy Evidence in Relation to Social Structure* (in the press).

E. A. WRIGLEY, 'Family Limitation in Pre-Industrial England', *Economic Statistical Review*, 1966.

P. LASLETT and J. HARISSA, *Clayworth and Cogenhoe. Historical Essays 1600–1750*, London, 1964.

D. V. GLASS and D. E. C. EVERSLEY (eds.), *Population in History. Essays in Historical Demography*, London, 1965.

T. H. HOLLINGSWORTH, *The Demography of the British Peerage*, London, The Population Investigation Committee, London School of Economics, n.d. (Supplement to *Population Studies* 18 (2).)

P. LASLETT, *The World We Have Lost*, London, 1965.

E. A. WRIGLEY, *London Population. Past and Present*, 1967.

At the University of California (Berkeley) can be cited the work of Messrs. BORAH, CIPOLLA and COOK.

155. At the University of Pennsylvania (Philadelphia), MR. JOHN DURAND is preparing a history of the world's population.

157. *Pierre de Boisguilbert ou la naissance de l'économie politique*, Paris, I.N.E.D., 1966, 2 vols.

161. *Methods of Estimating Basic Demographic Measures from Incomplete Data. Manual IV*, United Nations, 126 p. Tables, graphs. Sales no. 67.XIII.2.

162. *Age and Sex Patterns of Mortality. Model Life-Tables for Underdeveloped Countries*, United Nations, 1955 (ST/SOA/ Series A/22, Population Studies no. 22).

A. J. COALE and P. DEMENY, *Regional Model Life Tables and Stable Populations*, Princeton (N.J.), Princeton University Press, 1966.

–164. *The Concept of a Stable Population. Application to the Study of Populations of Countries with Incomplete Demographic Statistics*, United Nations, 1968 (ST/SOA/series A/39, Population Studies no. 39).

168. A. JACQUARD, 'La reproduction humaine en régime malthusien. Un modèle de simulation par la méthode de Monte-Carlo', *Population* (5), 1967, pp. 897–920.

J. C. RIDLEY and M. C. SHEPS, 'An Analytic Simulation Model of Human Reproduction with Demographic and Biological Components', *Population Studies* 19 (3), Mar. 1966, pp. 297–310.

170. R. BACHI, R. BARON and G. NATHAN, *Methods of Record-Linkage and Applications in Israel*. Paper (ref. 1/3) given at the 36th Session of the International Statistical Institute, Sydney (28 Aug.–7 Sept. 1967). Cf. Bibliography at the end of the paper.

171. Results of research on population genetics are published in the following journals:

Genetics. Official publication of the Genetics Society of America. University Station, Austin, Texas (U.S.A.).

Evolution (International Journal of Organic Evolution). Journal published by the Society for the Study of Evolution. Allen Press Inc., Lawrence, Kansas (U.S.A.).

Annals of Human Genetics. Galton Laboratory, University College, London. Bentley House, 200 Enston Road, London N.W.1.

American Journal of Human Genetics. Bimonthly journal published by the American Society of Human Genetics. Grune and Stratton, 81 Park Avenue South, New York, N.Y.

Population. Bimonthly journal published by the Institut national d'études démographiques. Editions de l'I.N.E.D., 23 avenue Franklin-Roosevelt, Paris VIIIe. See in particular in *Population* the following recent articles:
A. JACQUARD, 'Logique du calcul des coefficients d'identité entre deux individus', *Population* (4), July-Aug. 1966; 'Liaison génétique entre individus apparentés', *Population* (1), Jan.-Feb. 1968; 'Evolution des populations d'effectif limité', *Population* (2), Mar.-Apr. 1968.
A. JACQUARD and R. NADOT, 'Mariages consanguins et fertilité différentielle', *Population* (2), Mar.-Apr. 1968.
J. SUTTER, 'Fréquence de l'endogamie et ses facteurs au XIXème siècle', *Population* (2), Mar.-Apr. 1968. [At the end of this article is a long bibliography.]
J. SUTTER, 'Interprétation démographique de la fréquence des groupes sanguins chez les Wavena et les Emerillon de la Guyane', *Population* (4), July-Aug. 1967.

C. J. BAJEMA, 'Human Population Genetics and Demography: a Selected Bibliography', *Eugenics Quarterly* 14, 1967, pp. 205–237.

Demographic journals (both French and foreign):
C. LEGEARD, *Guide de recherches documentaires en démographie*, Paris, 1966, pp. 209–219.

Recently published works:
M. REINHARD, A. ARMENGAUD and J. DUPAQUIER, *Histoire générale de la population mondiale*, Paris, 1968.
E. SZABADY, *World Views of Population Problems*, Budapest, 1968.
J. HENRIPIN, *Tendances et facteurs de la fécondité au Canada*, Ottawa, Bureau Fédéral de la Statistique, 1968.
W. BRASS, A. J. COELE, P. DEMENY et al., *The Demography of Tropical Africa*, Princeton, 1968.
G. WOLSTENHOLME and M. O'CONNOR (eds.), *Health of Mankind*, London, 1967.

Index

Abortion, 14, 21, 64 *n*.11
adaptability, human, 42
Africa, 47, 48
age composition, 25–6, 56; of parents in procreation, 53
age-expectancy, 8
ageing process, 15, 18, 23, 62
aid, bilateral, 31; international, 31
alcohol, 20
anovular cycles, 15, 16, 53
answer-machine, 37
anthropology, French males, 59
Application of Science and Technology to Development, Advisory Committee, 48, 65 *n*.30
Argentina, 56
Asia, 47, 48, 63
Asian Drama: An Enquiry into the Poverty of Nations, 64 *n*.35
Atomic Age, 8
audio-visual media, 37
automation, 33
average laws, variance with, 9

behaviour, changes of, 9
bibliography *see* references
biological, aspects of fertility, 16, 52, 53, 54; development, 22, 24, 62; disorders, 18; phenomena *see* phenomena; urges, 8
biology, 11, 12–24, 52, 53; molecular, 24; pure, 24
Biometric Society, 45
biometrical survey, 51
birth control, 8, 54, 57, 58; *see also* contraceptives *and* family planning
births, 8, 9, 10, 11, 13, 33, 37, 38, 42; spacing of, 15, 17, 22, 24, 53
blood groups, 52
blood pressure, high, 20
Boisguilbert, 59
Boston, 58
brain-drain, 36
Brazil, 45–6
breast-feeding, 15, 52

Budapest, 46, 51, 58
Bureau of Labor Statistics (USA), 55

California, University of (Berkeley), 59
Cambridge Group for the History of Population and Social Structure, 58
Canada, 61
cancer, 19,20
Candau, Dr Marcolino, G., 65 *n*.32
capital, 28, 64 *n*.17, 64 *n*.19; income, 29, 64 *n*.17
Carnegie Endowment for International Peace, 49
celibacy, 16
census *see* population
Centro de Estudios Económicos y Demográficos, 56
chromosomes, 10, 14, 18, 52
civil registry, 39, 42, 44, 47, 65 *n*.24
civil status statistics, 9, 56, 63 *n*.3
civilization, 35
collectivities, 28, 29, 30
Comitato Italiano per lo Studio dei Problemi della Popolazione, 45
computers, 26, 35, 39, 40, 61, 64 *n*.22
conception, 13, 14, 18, 54, 64 *n*.12
conferences, 46, 47, 48, 50
congenital defects, 15, 52
consciousness, 10
consumption, patterns of, 25–6, 28, 30, 34, 56–7
contraceptives, 14, 16, 18, 22, 24, 41, 52, 54; law in France, 9, 64 *n*.4
Council of Europe, 48, 49
creation of the future, 11
criminology, 11
cultural system, 8
currency distribution, 29, 31, 32; on international scale, 31–2; *see also* money

Daedalus, 58
data, defective, 60–1; *see also* sample survey

Human Rights Conference, The, 33
Hungry, 51

infant mortality, 51
infanticide, 23, 64 *n*.10
infertility, 14, 15, 16, 22, 64 *n*.8
Institut de démographie of the University of Paris (IDUP), 46
Institut für empirische Soziologie at Nuremberg, 55
Institut national d'études démographiques (Paris), 45
Institute of Population Problems (Tokyo), 45
Instituto Balmes de Sociologia y Asociación para el Estudio Cientifico de los Problemas de Población (Spain), 45
Intergovernmental Committee for European Migration (ICEM), 48
International Biological Programme (IBP), 51
International Labour Office (ILO), 47, 57
international market, 30–2
International Statistical Institute (ISI), 45, 47
International Union for the Scientific Study of Population (IUSSP), 45, 53, 59
intra-uterine mortality, 13, 64 *n*.10
investment plan in economic development, 26, 32, 64 *n*.16
Italy, 45, 46, 58

Japan, 45–6, 55

Kerseboom, 59

Laboratorio de Estatistica (Brazil), 45
labour, force, 27–9, 30; market, 32; training, 27–8, 32–3
Latin America, 47, 48
law, 11
leisure, right to, 33
lethal equivalents, 62
life-expectancy, 11, 35
London School of Economics, 55, 65 *n*.36; Population Investigation Committee, 58
Lotka, Alfred J., 60
Louis XIV, 59

macro-economic angle, 54
Maison des sciences de l'homme, 50
Malécot, G. 62
Malthus, T. R., 62

man: and his environment, 34, *see also* environment; as consumer and producer, 24–6; mobility of, 28
marginal goods, 31
marriage, 8, 13, 22, 29, 37, 38, 42, 63 *n*.1, 64 *n*.7, 64 *n*.12; age, 13, 16; customs, 13, 39; 'situation', 39
mathematics, 11, 13, 27, 29, 41, 62
matter, 10; animate, 8, 10, 11; inanimate, 8, 11, 63 *n*.2; phenomena of *see* phenomena; study of, 7
medical care, 21, 33
medical science, 21
medicine, 11
megapolises, 36
'memory', 10, 19
menopause, 14, 32–4, 53
menstrual cycles, 15, 16
Metropolitan Life Insurance Company (USA), 52
Mexico, 55, 56
México, Colegio de, 56
migration, 13, 34, 35, 37, 56; differential, 13, 64 *n*.6
Millbank Memorial Fund, 45, 46, 49, 50, 56, 65 *n*.32, 65 *n*.33
miscarriage, 14, 52, 53
Moheau, 7
money, 24–5, 28, 30–1, 55; acquiring, 28, 30, 31; on international market, 31, 32
Mongolian child, 14
moral code, 8, 20
morbidity, 22, 52
mortality, 20–2, 42, 56; differential, 12, 51, 64 *n*.6; endogenous, 18, 23; exogenous, 18; genetic, 52; infant, 51; rate, 25, 51, 52, 57, 58, 59, 60, 64 *n*.10, 64 *n*.15
motivations: determining size of family, 53, 54; individual, 9, 40
Myrdal, G., 54

National Center for Health Statistics (USA), 51
National Committee on Maternal Health (USA), 54
National Health Survey (USA), 51
Neanderthal man, 8
needs: compared with possibilities, 26, 30; satisfaction of, 56, 65 *n*.37
neuro-endocrinology, 52
New York, 47
Northeastern University, Boston, 55

obesity, 20